PowerShell SysAdmin Crash Course

Second Edition

Unlock the Full Potential of PowerShell with Advanced Techniques, Automation, Configuration Management and Integration

Steeve Lee

Published by: GitforGits

Publisher: Sonal Dhandre

www.gitforgits.com

support@gitforgits.com

Printed in India

First Printing: January 2025

ISBN: 978-93-49174-96-2

Cover Design by: Kitten Publishing

Prologue

My name is Steeve Lee, and I'm excited to present the second edition of "PowerShell SysAdmin Crash Course." The first edition did better than I expected, and the great reviews and helpful feedback made it clear that people really liked it. That made me want to do even more to refine and expand the content. People loved the hands-on approach, and I took the suggestions to heart. They told me to add more practical examples and to cover more real-world scenarios. This edition builds on that success, offering deeper insights and additional techniques that I believe will change how you work with PowerShell.

In this book, I'll take you on a fundamentals exploration that quickly progresses to powerful, time-saving methods that can transform your day-to-day administrative tasks. I share my own experiences, challenges, and discoveries from the field, so you can see how PowerShell can be a true game-changer in managing IT environments. As you flip through the pages, you'll come across hands-on tasks like handling files, directories, and the registry, plus automating repetitive tasks with ease.

I've put a lot of real-world scenarios in this edition, based on what I've seen in my own career. You'll learn how to use PowerShell to manage multiple systems remotely, deploy updates, and monitor environments easily. I also explore ways to expand PowerShell's functionality, like creating custom modules and integrating it with modern automation tools. This book is designed to give you practical, hands-on examples that you can apply right away in your own workplace.

One thing I focused on was making the content as easy to access as possible. I made the explanations clear and straightforward, so even complex topics feel approachable. I also included a bunch of examples that you can try on your own. The whole point of the book is to help you build your confidence, step-by-step, from writing basic scripts to automating more complex tasks across different environments. Whether you're a pro or just getting started, you'll find techniques that'll help you get more done and make your daily operations more efficient.

I share the practical knowledge and best practices I've learned over the years. I'm a big believer in the power of automation and efficiency, and I'm excited to pass on the skills that have helped me solve real challenges in the field. I'm excited to hear how this edition helps you transform your system administration approach, and I hope you enjoy the journey.

My goal is to help you get the most out of PowerShell and make a real difference in your day-to-day management tasks.

Content

Preface

This second edition is a hands-on, practical book crafted to empower system administrators and PowerShell enthusiasts to efficiently perform everyday system administration tasks and to automate complex processes with confidence. This book will take you from the basics of PowerShell scripting to advanced techniques and beyond. You will gain hands-on experience with handling variables, data types, and loops while learning to create reliable scripts that manage files, folders, drives, and the Windows registry. You will be introduced to powerful features such as remoting, DSC, and integration with System Center Configuration Manager to ensure that you can manage and deploy configurations across distributed environments.

Additionally, the book covers the intersection of PowerShell with modern automation frameworks, including Ansible, Chef, Puppet, and popular CI/CD tools. Such integration helps you streamline deployments, orchestrate workflows, and maintain consistent configurations across Windows and cross-platform systems. It also covers advanced topics such as extending PowerShell through custom cmdlets, modules, and classes, as well as techniques to interact with external systems via RESTful APIs, Python, and Bash. With simple and straightforward examples, the book presents many aspects of system administration while also touching on more complex scenarios, giving you the insight you need to tackle challenging environments without overwhelming you.

In this book:

- You will be up and running with PowerShell scripting for system administration tasks.
- Use effective commands to manage files, folders, drives, and the Windows Registry.
- Use PowerShell remoting to securely manage multiple systems.
- Apply Desired State Configuration for automated, idempotent, and consistent infrastructure management.
- Integrate SCCM to automate deployments, software updates, and system configurations.
- Leverage advanced text manipulation with regular expressions for precise data extraction and transformation.
- Develop custom modules, cmdlets, and functions to effectively extend PowerShell's native capabilities.
- Employ multithreading and parallel processing to enhance script performance.
- Integrate PowerShell with Ansible, Chef, and Puppet.
- Safeguard PowerShell environments by implementing best practices, execution policies, and robust auditing techniques.

GitforGits

Prerequisites

This book is ideal for those who want to build a strong understanding of PowerShell and its application, from the basics to advanced techniques. It is also suitable for those who want to integrate PowerShell with automation and configuration management tools and other scripting languages.

Codes Usage

Are you in need of some helpful code examples to assist you in your programming and documentation? Look no further! Our book offers a wealth of supplemental material, including code examples and exercises.

Not only is this book here to aid you in getting your job done, but you have our permission to use the example code in your programs and documentation. However, please note that if you are reproducing a significant portion of the code, we do require you to contact us for permission.

But don't worry, using several chunks of code from this book in your program or answering a question by citing our book and quoting example code does not require permission. But if you do choose to give credit, an attribution typically includes the title, author, publisher, and ISBN. For example, "PowerShell SysAdmin Crash Course, Second Edition by Steeve Lee".

If you are unsure whether your intended use of the code examples falls under fair use or the permissions outlined above, please do not hesitate to reach out to us at support@gitforgits.com.

We are happy to assist and clarify any concerns.

Acknowledgement

I owe a tremendous debt of gratitude to GitforGits, for their unflagging enthusiasm and wise counsel throughout the entire process of writing this book. Their knowledge and careful editing helped make sure the piece was useful for people of all reading levels and comprehension skills. In addition, I'd like to thank everyone involved in the publishing process for their efforts in making this book a reality. Their efforts, from copyediting to advertising, made the project what it is today.

Finally, I'd like to express my gratitude to everyone who has shown me unconditional love and encouragement throughout my life. Their support was crucial to the completion of this book. I appreciate your help with this endeavour and your continued interest in my career.

Chapter 1: Beginning with PowerShell

Chapter Overview

In this chapter, you'll get a hands-on understanding of PowerShell's role in modern system administration and automation. You'll see how it processes data as objects, making filtering and sorting easier than with traditional text-based shells. You'll also learn the main differences between PowerShell and the Command Prompt. This will help you understand why PowerShell's object-oriented model offers more flexibility for complex tasks.

We'll also dive into the different PowerShell editions and how each one handles unique tasks, from Windows-centric management to cross-platform scenarios. Then, we'll dive into PowerShell's history, starting from its early versions and working up to the latest release. You'll see how the language has expanded its capabilities and gained cross-platform support over time. We'll also go over how to install it on Linux, including how to get the official packages and make sure everything's set up right. The code examples illustrate how to check versions, retrieve processes, and create pipelines that manipulate data in real time. You'll also get a sense of how PowerShell's ecosystem is always changing by looking at modules that add new features.

By the time this chapter's over, you'll be all set to use PowerShell 7.3 on Linux, and you'll enjoy a consistent approach to automation that'll bring diverse environments together.

What is PowerShell?

A surge in the demand for efficient automation and streamlined system administration has propelled tools like PowerShell into the spotlight. You might have noticed how industries and IT departments lean on automation to manage complex infrastructures without the constant need for manual intervention. Automation scripting tools have become indispensable because they offer the means to reduce repetitive tasks, simplify configurations, and enable rapid deployment of critical updates across diverse environments. As organizations expand and technology evolves, you will find that PowerShell's ability to handle multifaceted tasks with a single, cohesive language makes it a top pick for professionals seeking to boost productivity and accuracy in system management. Its design addresses the need for a reliable tool that can be applied in both small-scale operations and large enterprise environments, allowing you to focus on strategic initiatives while routine tasks run seamlessly in the background.

Essence of PowerShell

You encounter PowerShell when you require a tool that not only automates tasks but also integrates deeply with system components, whether you are managing file systems, interacting with network services, or configuring applications. The foundation of PowerShell lies in its integration with the .NET Framework on Windows and .NET Core for its cross-platform iterations, equipping you with access to a robust array of management tools and APIs. This integration ensures that when you write scripts, you are working with powerful system management capabilities that enhance your ability to solve real-world challenges.

A noticeable trend in modern IT practices is the widespread adoption of automation scripting tools. Organizations around the globe rely on PowerShell because it significantly minimizes the margin of error that comes with manual intervention and enhances the overall efficiency of system administration. You may have experienced moments where manual tasks were not only time-consuming but also error-prone, leading to unexpected downtimes or security lapses. In contrast, PowerShell brings consistency and repeatability to your operations. Its object-oriented nature means that each command interacts with structured data, making it easier for you to process, filter, and manipulate information without the typical hassles associated with text-based processing. When you implement PowerShell in your environment, you are not just adopting a scripting language; you are stepping into a framework that supports scalability, reliability, and streamlined operations that modern enterprises demand.

Core Features of PowerShell

PowerShell has a bunch of features that make it super easy to manage complex systems. One of the best parts is its huge set of built-in cmdlets. These cmdlets are like modules that you can mix and match to do more complex tasks, and they follow a simple verb-noun naming system that makes it easy to figure out and use the commands you need. The built-in help system and online resources make it easy to find detailed instructions and examples, so you won't have to struggle to learn how to use it. With over 600 built-in cmdlets, you've got the tools you need to handle everything from file management to network configuration.

Let us understand the core fetures that make PowerShell strong and robust tool in the following:

Object-Oriented Approach

PowerShell distinguishes itself by treating data as objects rather than mere text. This object-oriented paradigm gives you the flexibility to interact with data in a structured format, which proves essential when you are required to filter, sort, or manipulate output in intricate ways. For instance, when you run a command to list system processes, you receive objects that contain properties and methods. This arrangement allows you to effortlessly extract only the necessary information, apply filters, or even perform further actions on those objects without additional processing.

Pipeline Mastery

Another feature that enhances your scripting experience is the pipeline. The pipeline enables you to take the output of one cmdlet and use it as the input for another, which not only simplifies your code but also allows you to perform multi-step operations in a single command sequence. With the pipeline, you are empowered to build commands that process data in a fluid manner, chaining operations together without the need for intermediary storage or additional scripting overhead.

Modular Architecture

PowerShell's support for modules means you can extend its capabilities to suit your unique needs. Modules are collections of cmdlets, functions, and scripts that bundle related functionalities together. Whether you rely on built-in modules provided by Microsoft or develop custom modules to address specific tasks, you benefit from a design that encourages reuse and organized code. You will often appreciate how modules facilitate collaboration in team environments by providing standardized tools and methods for managing systems.

Scripting and Remoting Capabilities

The scripting features of PowerShell are engineered to make automation accessible and efficient. When you write scripts in PowerShell, you have the full arsenal of programming constructs available—loops, conditionals, error handling, and more. This allows you to build robust solutions that adapt to changing system states. Moreover, PowerShell's remoting capabilities mean that you can manage tasks across multiple systems from a single console. This remote management is vital when you oversee a network of machines, enabling you to administer commands on different systems without having to physically access each one.

Customization and Extensibility

A notable strength of PowerShell lies in its high degree of customization. You are given the freedom to create custom cmdlets and functions tailored to your environment. This extensibility means that as your organization's needs evolve, your scripting language can evolve alongside them. Whether you integrate third-party modules or develop bespoke solutions, PowerShell's open design allows you to push its capabilities beyond what comes out of the box. In environments where rapid changes occur, such flexibility ensures that your tools remain relevant and effective.

Cross-Platform and Security Considerations

PowerShell has grown beyond its initial Windows-only design. The availability of PowerShell Core on Linux and macOS expands the scope of its application, making it an ideal choice for managing heterogeneous environments. When you work in a cross-platform setting, you enjoy a unified scripting language that operates consistently across different operating systems. In addition to its versatility, PowerShell incorporates robust security features. Execution policies, constrained language modes, and just enough administration (JEA) provide a layered security approach, allowing you to control who executes scripts and how they interact with the system. These features play a vital role in safeguarding systems against unauthorized access or accidental misuse.

Embracing the Power of PowerShell

A careful examination of PowerShell reveals a tool that is built with your operational needs in mind. Its ease of use, paired with an extensive feature set, makes it an appealing option for anyone who seeks to bring automation into their daily work routines. You experience the benefit of fewer manual interventions, a lower likelihood of errors, and a smoother workflow overall. With PowerShell, you step into a world where repetitive tasks are handled automatically, freeing your time to focus on strategic initiatives and innovation within your organization. The clear object orientation, modular architecture, and secure, cross-platform design ensure that you have a versatile tool that scales with your needs and grows in tandem with technological advancements.

PowerShell vs. Command Prompt

PowerShell's got a ton of features that make managing complex systems a breeze. One of the best parts is its huge set of built-in cmdlets. These modules let you mix and match them to do more complex tasks, and they follow a simple verb-noun naming system that makes it easy to figure out and use the commands you need. It's also got a built-in help system and online resources that make it a breeze to find detailed instructions and examples, so you won't have to struggle to figure it out. With over 600 cmdlets at your fingertips, you've got everything you need to handle everything from filing to network configuration.

Data Processing

A major distinction between the two tools lies in the way they process data. Command Prompt treats every piece of output as plain text. You might face challenges when you need to extract or filter specific information from a block of text, which often requires additional tools or custom scripting. In contrast, PowerShell processes data as objects. This object-oriented approach means that every command you execute returns structured data, complete with properties and methods. When you work with PowerShell, you have the ability to interact with data in a granular manner—filtering, sorting, and even performing mathematical operations without cumbersome text manipulation.

Command Handling and Syntax

Another aspect where you notice a clear divide is in command handling. Command Prompt relies on a relatively small set of built-in commands, requiring you to remember specific syntaxes and often turn to external utilities to accomplish more advanced tasks. PowerShell, on the other hand, boasts a vast array of built-in cmdlets that follow a consistent verb-noun naming convention. This consistency allows you to intuitively understand and predict the function of a cmdlet simply by its name. When you learn a few core commands, the pattern becomes easy to follow, and you quickly extend that knowledge to a wide variety of tasks.

Pipeline and Data Flow

The pipeline feature in PowerShell deserves special attention. When you chain commands together, you create a seamless flow of data from one operation to the next. You notice that by passing objects through the pipeline, each stage of your script can operate on the structured output of the previous command. This not only simplifies the scripting process but also enhances the performance of your commands by reducing the need for intermediate storage or manual parsing.

Ease of Use and Learning Curve

When you evaluate both tools in terms of user-friendliness, PowerShell tends to stand out. Its clear syntax and interactive help system lower the barriers to entry for newcomers. You have access to a rich set of online resources that illustrate command usage, error handling, and best practices in a way that is accessible and relatable. Although Command Prompt may appear straightforward at first glance, its limitations quickly become apparent as tasks grow in complexity. In contrast, the learning curve of PowerShell is mitigated by its logical structure and consistency, which enable you to gradually build your skills while accomplishing real-world tasks efficiently.

Interactive Features and Customization

In Command Prompt, customization is often limited to changing window colors or fonts, with little opportunity to extend functionality without third-party tools. PowerShell's environment, however, allows you to tailor both the interface and the functionality to suit your needs. By creating custom functions, aliases, and modules, you build an ecosystem that evolves alongside your operational requirements. You experience a system where every tweak and addition is designed to enhance your productivity and streamline your workflow. The ability to integrate with other tools and services, combined with PowerShell's inherent extensibility, offers a level of customization that Command Prompt simply cannot match.

Operational Benefit

As you transition from using Command Prompt to PowerShell, you notice improvements in productivity and accuracy. PowerShell's modern design addresses many of the shortcomings of its predecessor. With its ability to handle remote sessions, secure operations, and manage cross-platform tasks, you gain access to a tool that is versatile enough to meet the demands of today's complex IT environments. Your daily administrative tasks become more streamlined, and you benefit from a reduction in the time spent on repetitive, manual tasks. The operational efficiency that comes with PowerShell can significantly impact how you manage your systems, leading to a more organized and responsive IT infrastructure.

When you adopt PowerShell over Command Prompt, you embrace a tool that not only meets the challenges of modern system administration but also anticipates future needs. The shift to an object-oriented and pipeline-driven environment is more than a change in syntax; it represents a fundamental evolution in how you approach automation and system management. You discover that the interactivity, flexibility, and depth of customization provided by PowerShell empower you to tackle tasks that were once cumbersome or time-consuming.

PowerShell Editions and Versions

A variety of PowerShell editions exists because organizations often manage diverse environments that extend beyond traditional Windows desktops and servers. You may have a scenario where Linux systems, macOS endpoints, and cloud services must all be handled with a single scripting language. The different editions of PowerShell cater to these distinct needs by providing specialized modules and configurations for each platform or service. It gives you the flexibility to install the edition that aligns with your primary use case or combine multiple editions if you operate across varied infrastructures. Each edition adheres to the same PowerShell language principles, so your knowledge remains transferable. It becomes easier to shift from Windows PowerShell to PowerShell Core or even to Azure PowerShell without feeling like you are learning an entirely different tool. The unifying factor is the common scripting foundation that underpins all editions, ensuring that your skills stay relevant.

Windows PowerShell

Windows PowerShell emerged as the original implementation of PowerShell, introduced around the release of Windows Vista. This edition was built on the .NET Framework and rapidly became an integral part of Windows operating systems, making it a go-to choice for many professionals. You might have encountered Windows PowerShell if you have ever administered a Windows Server environment or automated tasks in a Windows domain. It excels in managing Windows-specific features like the Registry, Active Directory, and WMI. One reason for its popularity is the extensive set of cmdlets that tackle common Windows administrative tasks without requiring external utilities. This built-in nature saves time when you are juggling multiple projects, since you can rely on consistent, native tools. While Windows PowerShell remains widely used, newer editions now exist to address cross-platform scenarios and cloud-based services, prompting some users to consider transitioning to more modern alternatives.

PowerShell Core

A desire to manage Linux and macOS systems with the same scripting language led Microsoft to create PowerShell Core. You might opt for PowerShell Core when you oversee environments that mix Windows and non-Windows systems. This edition relies on .NET Core rather than the full .NET Framework, giving it the ability to run seamlessly on multiple platforms. The command set you encounter is mostly aligned with Windows PowerShell, so scripts you developed in one environment can often be adapted to another with minimal changes. Cross-platform functionality can be pivotal if your organization has embraced open-source solutions or if you prefer to unify administrative tasks under a single shell. Although PowerShell Core initially lacked some modules found in Windows PowerShell, improvements over time have narrowed that gap. You benefit from a more consistent experience across diverse systems, creating an efficient workflow that transcends operating system boundaries.

Azure PowerShell

Organizations increasingly move resources to the cloud, and Azure PowerShell addresses that shift by focusing on Azure-based services. If you are responsible for deploying virtual machines, configuring storage, or orchestrating networking in Microsoft Azure, Azure PowerShell can become a significant asset. Its modules are specifically tailored to automate tasks in the Azure ecosystem, allowing you to script everything from initial resource group creation to advanced tasks like configuring virtual networks or deploying container instances. It grants a high level of control over cloud resources, enabling you to scale deployments and maintain configurations with ease. Azure PowerShell often integrates well with other editions of PowerShell, so you can manage on-premises Windows systems, Linux servers, and Azure resources from one interface. You gain a powerful means of bridging your local data center with the cloud, ensuring consistent practices across all environments.

Exchange Server PowerShell

Many organizations rely on Microsoft Exchange for email and collaboration. You may find yourself juggling mailbox creation, distribution group management, and permission configurations on a daily basis. Exchange Server PowerShell addresses these needs by offering specialized modules and cmdlets that simplify tasks within Exchange environments. Rather than navigating through graphical consoles or manually modifying configurations, you can automate repetitive procedures with scripts. For instance, the ability to create mailboxes in bulk or adjust mailbox quotas for a specific group of users becomes more straightforward when you leverage dedicated cmdlets. It often results in a more consistent configuration state across your organization. Exchange Server PowerShell also opens up the possibility of integrating email-related tasks with broader administrative scripts, so you can unify daily routines in a single, efficient workflow. This synergy reduces overhead and fosters consistency in email management.

SharePoint Server PowerShell

SharePoint Server is frequently used for document management, team collaboration, and content organization. You might be tasked with setting up new sites, configuring libraries, or managing user permissions on a platform that is central to business operations. SharePoint Server PowerShell simplifies these processes by offering a set of cmdlets that address the unique structures and features within SharePoint. Activities such as site creation, list configuration, and user management can be automated, saving significant time when you administer multiple sites or handle large numbers of users. SharePoint Server PowerShell also integrates well with broader PowerShell strategies, allowing you to combine SharePoint tasks with system or network operations in a unified script. This capability is especially helpful if your environment requires frequent changes or expansions, ensuring that you can replicate configurations quickly while minimizing manual steps. The specialized focus of these cmdlets offers a consistent method of working with SharePoint's extensive feature set.

The variety of PowerShell editions highlights the versatility and adaptability of this scripting environment. You are free to select the edition that best suits your operational requirements, whether that means running cross-platform scripts with PowerShell Core or focusing on cloud deployments with Azure PowerShell. Specialized editions like Exchange Server PowerShell and SharePoint Server PowerShell cater to the unique needs of administrators in those fields, streamlining processes that might otherwise be cumbersome. Although each edition has a distinct focus, the underlying PowerShell language remains familiar. This unified scripting foundation enables you to build a cohesive toolkit for managing every layer of your environment, from on-premises Windows systems to modern cloud infrastructures. The alignment across editions reduces the time spent learning different tools and fosters a deeper mastery of PowerShell as a whole.

PowerShell Versions

PowerShell 1 and 2

Microsoft's introduction of Windows PowerShell 1.0 in 2006 marked a pivotal change in how Windows administrators approached system management. You might recall a time when Command Prompt was the default option, and batch files were the primary way to automate tasks. Windows PowerShell 1.0 provided an entirely new experience by treating data as objects, offering a pipeline for chaining commands, and delivering a more robust scripting language. This initial release already included a substantial collection of cmdlets that simplified common tasks, such as managing files and services. Although it lacked the depth and polish of later versions, Windows PowerShell 1.0 laid the groundwork for what would become a thriving ecosystem. You might have encountered it in environments that were beginning to adopt automation, serving as a testbed for the advanced features that would appear in subsequent releases.

A few years after the version 1, Windows PowerShell 2.0 arrived with significant enhancements. One of the most notable additions was the PowerShell Integrated Scripting Environment (ISE), which gave you a dedicated workspace to write, run, and debug scripts. Remoting capabilities were also introduced, enabling you to execute commands on remote systems without physically logging in to each machine. This feature revolutionized how large-scale environments were managed, allowing centralized administration for fleets of servers. Another improvement was the concept of modules, which offered a more organized way to distribute cmdlets and functions. You likely appreciated how modules allowed you to group related functionalities together, making it easier to share your work with colleagues. Windows PowerShell 2.0 built upon the core principles introduced in version 1.0, setting the stage for more advanced features in the pipeline.

PowerShell 3 and 4

The release of Windows PowerShell 3.0 saw the arrival of workflows, a powerful addition that addressed the need for long-running or parallelized tasks. You may have found workflows particularly useful in scenarios where processes spanned multiple machines or took a significant amount of time to complete. PowerShell's remoting capabilities received further refinements, making it more reliable for managing distributed environments. Another improvement was the streamlined syntax for common operations, reducing the verbosity of scripts and enabling you to accomplish tasks with fewer lines of code. The module ecosystem also expanded, bringing more specialized modules for tasks like Active Directory management or networking configurations. Windows PowerShell 3.0 represented a turning point, as it demonstrated the language's growing maturity and adaptability to complex enterprise needs. You could automate large-scale tasks with greater confidence and fewer workarounds.

Then an important leap came when Windows PowerShell 4.0 came into use, which introduced Desired State Configuration (DSC). This feature addressed the challenge of maintaining a consistent configuration across multiple systems, allowing you to define a desired state for each machine and ensure that it remained in compliance. DSC's declarative approach meant you could specify the end goal, and PowerShell would handle the implementation details. It is a simplified large-scale deployment, as it eliminated many of the manual steps once required to align system configurations. Windows PowerShell 4.0 also introduced improvements in debugging, letting you troubleshoot scripts more effectively. This version made the language more accessible to administrators who wanted advanced management features without writing overly complicated code. You might have found that DSC quickly became a cornerstone of modern DevOps practices, allowing smoother collaboration between development and operations teams.

PowerShell 5 and 5.1

Windows PowerShell 5.0 introduced a significant milestone by unveiling the PowerShell Gallery, an online repository that allowed you to find and share modules and scripts more easily. This development fostered a sense of community around PowerShell, as administrators and developers alike could contribute useful code to a shared library. PowerShell 5.0 and 5.1 also included enhancements such as class-based programming, which gave you an object-oriented way to structure scripts and modules. This addition bridged the gap between scripting and traditional software development, making PowerShell more appealing to those with a background in languages like C#. Windows Management Framework updates ensured that these newer versions could run on older Windows systems, enabling you to standardize your automation tools even if your infrastructure spanned multiple OS versions. These releases further cemented Windows PowerShell as a robust platform for enterprise automation.

PowerShell 6

A significant shift occurred with the introduction of PowerShell 6, which marked the transition to an open-source, cross-platform model known as PowerShell Core. This move was driven by the desire to unify administration across Windows, Linux, and macOS. You might have been initially cautious about whether your existing scripts would run seamlessly, but many found that most commands worked similarly, thanks to a concerted effort to maintain backward compatibility. PowerShell 6 embraced .NET Core, providing a lighter and more modular framework. This cross-platform approach helped you avoid juggling multiple scripting solutions for different operating systems. Although some Windows-specific features were not immediately available, the open-source community worked diligently to fill those gaps. By adopting PowerShell 6, you took a step toward a more unified future, where a single scripting language could manage a heterogeneous infrastructure.

PowerShell 7, 7.1, 7.2, and 7.3

The PowerShell 7 family builds upon the groundwork of PowerShell 6, offering refinements, improved performance, and expanded compatibility with existing Windows PowerShell modules. You likely appreciate how these newer versions address feature gaps, ensuring that Windows-specific modules and advanced functionalities are accessible even in a cross-platform context. PowerShell 7.3 continues this trend, incorporating updates that enhance stability, security, and overall user experience. The community-driven nature of these releases means that bug fixes and feature requests are addressed more rapidly, giving you a scripting environment that evolves in step with real-world needs. The addition of parallelization improvements, better error handling, and refined remoting capabilities demonstrates an ongoing commitment to making PowerShell a comprehensive management tool.

Installing PowerShell

You might already be familiar with native Linux shells like Bash or Zsh and wonder why you would add another shell to your toolbox. PowerShell brings an object-oriented approach, a consistent command naming convention, and access to modules that can simplify a variety of tasks. It can run scripts that target cloud services, on-premises resources, or remote systems, all from within a single shell. This flexibility means you can write or reuse scripts that were originally created for Windows-centric environments while enjoying the advantages of Linux-based infrastructure. A growing number of professionals have discovered that PowerShell on Linux not only consolidates their scripting efforts but also streamlines the automation of cross-platform projects.

Access to PowerShell 7.3 Packages

A direct route to installing PowerShell 7.3 on many Linux distributions is to use the Microsoft repositories. This method gives you an official package that stays up-to-date with the latest security patches and feature enhancements. You avoid the hassle of building from source or manually updating binaries. Before proceeding, you might want to check the version of your Linux distribution to confirm compatibility with the PowerShell package. An example would be Ubuntu 20.04 or higher, which is widely used and receives full support for PowerShell installations. A typical approach involves downloading and registering the Microsoft GPG keys, adding the PowerShell repository to your package manager, and then installing the PowerShell package. Each of these steps can be carried out in a terminal session without needing additional configuration files or advanced manual tweaks. It ensures a stable, predictable experience that aligns with common Linux administrative practices.

Installing PowerShell Package

An Ubuntu-based system often serves as a good illustration of how to install PowerShell from the official Microsoft repositories. You may begin by opening a terminal window and updating your package lists with the apt-get update command. Once your package lists are refreshed, the next step is to install the prerequisites that enable your system to securely connect to Microsoft's repositories. These prerequisites can include packages like curl, software-properties-common, or gnupg if they are not already installed.

A sample command sequence for Ubuntu might look like this:

```
sudo apt-get update

sudo apt-get install -y wget apt-transport-https software-
properties-common

wget -q
https://packages.microsoft.com/config/ubuntu/20.04/packages-
microsoft-prod.deb

sudo dpkg -i packages-microsoft-prod.deb

sudo apt-get update

sudo apt-get install -y powershell
```

You begin by updating the local apt cache, then install some necessary packages for secure downloads and repository management. The next steps involve fetching the Microsoft repository configuration file and installing it using dpkg. An additional apt-get update ensures that your system recognizes the newly added repository. Finally, you install the powershell package, which places the pwsh executable on your system.

Verifying Install

Now to verify, you may simply begin by typing pwsh --version in your terminal, which should display the version number, such as 7.3.x, indicating that PowerShell 7.3 is active on your system. Another option is to simply type pwsh to launch a PowerShell session, where you can test a basic command like Get-Location or Get-Process. Although those commands are originally from a Windows-centric environment, they run seamlessly on Linux with object-oriented output. You might also run $PSVersionTable to view a detailed table of version information, including the edition (Core) and other relevant properties.

An illustrative example of a practical task involves retrieving system information through

PowerShell on Linux. You might launch a PowerShell session by typing pwsh, then run a command that lists processes, memory usage, or disk utilization. A sample command to list processes might look like this:

```
Get-Process | Select-Object -First 10
```

This command returns an object-oriented list of the first ten processes, showing properties such as CPU usage, process ID, and memory consumption. A Linux-based user accustomed to text-based commands like ps might appreciate how PowerShell allows immediate filtering, sorting, or additional processing of that data. If you want to filter by a specific process name, you can pipe the output to Where-Object:

```
Get-Process | Where-Object { $_.ProcessName -eq "bash" }
```

This command locates any running process named "bash." The combination of object-based output and flexible pipelines demonstrates how PowerShell merges Windows-style cmdlets with the Linux environment. You benefit from being able to adapt scripts across different operating systems while retaining the same command structures.

Summary

The first chapter gave the lowdown on PowerShell, which is a cross-platform shell and scripting language developed by Microsoft. It highlighted its object-oriented design, the pipeline feature, and the modular architecture that allows users to manage both local and remote environments efficiently. It also explained the differences between PowerShell and the Command Prompt, showing how PowerShell handles data as objects instead of plain text. This makes filtering, sorting, and managing output way more efficient. The chapter also talked about different PowerShell versions, like Windows PowerShell, PowerShell Core, and specialized versions like Azure PowerShell, Exchange Server PowerShell, and SharePoint Server PowerShell. It also talked about how PowerShell has evolved from version 1.0 to 7.3, highlighting improvements like remote access, Desired State Configuration, and cross-platform compatibility. It showed how these updates made admin tasks easier, cut down on manual interventions, and supported modern DevOps practices.

The final sections covered installing PowerShell on Linux and launching it, checking the version, and running cmdlets that retrieved process information. The chapter gave us some great insights into integrating PowerShell into existing workflows to handle all kinds of scenarios. People found out how modules added to PowerShell's functionality. The output made it so that automation was more fluid.

CHAPTER 2: POWERSHELL BASICS

Chapter Overview

This chapter will walk you through the main ideas of PowerShell Basics, giving you a deep dive into the practical and theoretical sides of the language. You'll learn how to set up the PowerShell console to create a personalized workspace that boosts your productivity and makes repetitive tasks a breeze. You'll learn how to set up your profile, where you can define aliases, functions, and variables that load automatically, saving you time every time you start a session.

Next, you will dive into the syntax and grammar of PowerShell and learn to build scripts from the ground up by working with variables, strings, arrays, conditional statements, loops, and functions. With the help of real-world examples and code snippets, you will get the hands-on experience you need to apply these concepts in real-world scenarios. As you go through it, you'll see how each part of PowerShell comes together to make a scripting language that's both versatile and powerful, great for automating complex tasks.

Configuring PowerShell Console

PowerShell's got a lot to offer right away. The moment you launch the console, you'll see how easy it is to get the look and feel of the environment just right for your workflow. You've already been introduced to PowerShell in the previous chapter, and now you find that version 7.3 brings enhancements that make configuring the console even more compelling. It's not just a regular terminal window; it adapts into a personalized command center that's always there to meet your needs.

Adjusting Appearance and Behavior

When you open the PowerShell console, a first step involves customizing its appearance and behavior. You can start by right-clicking the title bar and selecting “Properties” (or “Defaults” if you want settings to apply to all future sessions). A dialogue appears with multiple tabs that let you modify settings such as font type, font size, colors, and window layout. You might choose a monospaced font with a larger size to improve clarity and enable font smoothing for a more refined look. The “Colors” tab offers you control over the foreground and background hues, so you create a color scheme that suits your visual comfort during long coding sessions.

On the “Options” tab, features like QuickEdit mode become available, letting you quickly select and copy text without needing external shortcuts. You also adjust the command history size, which proves invaluable when you’re iterating over commands in a session.

Tweaking Layout and Buffer Settings

The “Layout” tab presents you with options to adjust the window size and buffer dimensions. You might set a wider buffer if you plan to scroll through extensive output or a custom window position that fits neatly on your screen. These adjustments prove essential when dealing with long scripts or when monitoring real-time logs. The window title can be customized too, enabling you to reflect your project name or a motivational phrase that keeps you focused.

When you complete these adjustments and confirm your changes, the changes extend beyond appearance; they enhance usability. For instance, a larger buffer ensures that you capture all necessary output, while a customized font aids readability, especially when dealing with complex command outputs or debugging sessions.

PowerShell 7.3 Enhancements

PowerShell 7.3 has introduced subtle improvements that influence how the console behaves. You might notice that error messages appear with enhanced clarity and that tab completions are more accurate and context-aware. The console now integrates better with modern system themes and supports Unicode more seamlessly, which is particularly useful if you work with internationalized data or scripts containing special characters.

You may also explore the new command-line parameters in version 7.3. For example, launching PowerShell with specific startup scripts or modules preloaded can further streamline your session. These parameters allow you to set a default profile or even open multiple tabs in a single instance when running PowerShell in environments like Windows Terminal.

With PowerShell 7.3, some settings have become easier to change on the fly. You begin to view the console as more than just a place to type commands—it becomes an extension of your workspace. The time spent fine-tuning these settings results in a smoother experience, as each setting you adjust contributes to a working environment that feels efficient and comfortable.

Customize PowerShell Profile

The next step in your learning with PowerShell is to customize your profile. It is a powerful feature that lets you define your environment every time you open the console. The profile is a script that runs when you open the console, setting up aliases, functions, variables, and even importing modules that you use regularly. With PowerShell 7.3, this process stays simple but now gives you more flexibility and performance.

Creating and Editing Profile

To customize your PowerShell profile, you start by opening a terminal session and typing the command:

```
notepad $PROFILE
```

This command opens your profile file in Notepad. If the file does not exist, you receive a prompt asking whether to create a new file. By accepting, you set the stage for defining your customizations.

Defining Aliases and Functions

In the profile, you can define aliases that simplify frequently used commands. For instance, you can create an alias so that typing "ll" executes the command to list all files (including hidden ones):

```
Set-Alias ll Get-ChildItem -Force
```

This alias streamlines your workflow, reducing keystrokes and making common operations more intuitive. You also have the opportunity to define functions that encapsulate more complex tasks. Let us think of a function that checks the status of a website. For this, you might write:

```
function Get-WebsiteStatus {
    try {
        $response = Invoke-WebRequest -Uri
"https://www.example.com" -UseBasicParsing
        if ($response.StatusCode -eq 200) {
            Write-Host "The website is up and running."
        }
    }
    catch {
        Write-Host "The website is down or unreachable."
    }
}
```

This function makes use of a try-catch block to handle potential errors, reflecting best practices in PowerShell 7.3. You experience a smoother operation when functions are preloaded; each time you open the console, these capabilities are immediately available.

Setting Variables and Importing Modules

You might define variables in your profile to store paths or configuration settings that you use repeatedly. For example:

```
$WorkspacePath = "C:\Users\YourUserName\Documents\Projects"
```

With this variable defined, you streamline navigation and script execution. Additionally, you can import modules that enhance your PowerShell experience. For instance, if you frequently work with Azure resources, you can add:

```
Import-Module Az
```

This command ensures that the Azure module loads automatically, letting you run cloud management commands without extra steps. In PowerShell 7.3, module loading has been optimized to reduce startup delays, giving you quick access to essential tools.

Customizing Prompt

Another interesting aspect of the profile is the ability to customize the command prompt. You might choose to modify the prompt function to display useful information such as the current directory or even the time. An example customization might look like this:

```
function Prompt {
    $currentPath = Get-Location
    Write-Host "PS [$currentPath]>" -NoNewline -
ForegroundColor Cyan
    return " "
}
```

This customization helps you stay oriented during long sessions and ensures that important context remains visible at all times. And, the visual cues provided by a customized prompt can significantly enhance your efficiency.

Testing Customizations

After saving your profile, you close the editor and restart the PowerShell console to see your customizations in effect. You might run a few test commands to confirm that aliases, functions, and prompt modifications behave as expected. If adjustments are needed, you return to the profile file, edit the relevant lines, and save the changes.

You will be quickly noticing that a well-crafted profile reduces repetitive tasks and creates a consistent working environment. Each time you open the console, you benefit from a setup that is tailored to your needs, whether you are managing system configurations, developing scripts, or interacting with cloud services. The profile not only enhances efficiency but also fosters a sense of ownership over your tools. Every time you customize the PowerShell profile, you unlock new possibilities for automation and integration with other tools. This practice transforms routine operations into a seamless process that accelerates your productivity.

PowerShell Syntax and Grammar

Let us now explore the essential building blocks of PowerShell i.e. syntax and grammar. We previously learned that variables in PowerShell are created simply by assigning a value to a name prefixed with a dollar sign. For example, the command

```
$greeting = "Hello, PowerShell 7.3!"
Write-Output $greeting
```

displays a message that confirms the variable's content. You can see that strings are treated as text enclosed in quotes, which can be combined or manipulated using built-in operators and methods.

Similarly, the arrays are defined by listing items separated by commas:

```
$colors = "Red", "Green", "Blue"
Write-Output $colors[1]
```

This outputs the second element of the array. We can also leverage conditional statements with the if construct to compare variable values as below:

```
$name = "Alice"
if ($name -eq "Alice") {
    Write-Output "Hello, Alice!"
} else {
    Write-Output "Who are you?"
}
```

This conditional logic provides us with a means to execute code selectively. We can construct loops using for and while constructs to perform repetitive tasks. For example, in a for loop, we can iterate through a range of values:

```
for ($i = 0; $i -lt 5; $i++) {
    Write-Output "Count: $i"
}
```

and in a while loop, we maintain the similar functionality with a different structure:

```
$i = 0
while ($i -lt 5) {
    Write-Output "Count: $i"
    $i++
```

```
}
```

Also, the functions in PowerShell encapsulates reusable logic. For instance, let us define a function that adds two numbers:

```
function Add-Numbers {
    param($num1, $num2)
    $sum = $num1 + $num2
    Write-Output "The sum of $num1 and $num2 is: $sum"
}
Add-Numbers -num1 10 -num2 15
```

This function shows how parameter input and output could be structured effectively. We can experiment with advanced features such as script blocks, error handling with try-catch, and here-strings for multiline text.

Summary

To sum it up, we learned a lot from this chapter and it really changed the way we do things. You tried things out with the PowerShell Console, changing how it looked, optimizing buffer sizes, and setting up behavior options that improved how interactive it was. You also customized your profile by defining aliases, functions, and variables that automatically loaded each time the console started, thereby streamlining repetitive tasks.

You also got into the nitty-gritty of PowerShell syntax and grammar, learning to create and manipulate variables, strings, arrays, and control structures like if statements, loops, and functions. This hands-on experience gave you a solid foundation in both the practical and theoretical aspects of PowerShell scripting. By working through interactive examples and code snippets, you gained valuable insights that improved your ability to automate tasks and manage environments efficiently.

CHAPTER 3: CMDLETS, ALIASES, AND FUNCTIONS

Chapter Overview

This chapter will teach you the basics of PowerShell scripting, focusing on cmdlets, aliases, and functions. You'll start by learning what cmdlets are and how their standardized naming conventions make tasks easier to understand and use. We'll take a look at 25 popular cmdlets with some practical examples, and you'll see how they can be used as building blocks for your automation projects.

Then, we'll dive into creating and managing aliases to make your workflow more efficient. After that, we'll go into detail about defining and using functions to build reusable code blocks. As you go through it, you'll learn some basic and more advanced techniques, like how to validate parameters and handle errors. By the time you're done, you'll be able to write solid, efficient scripts. This chapter's going to give you the hands-on skills you need to get the most out of PowerShell in your day-to-day work.

Exploring Cmdlets

Cmdlets are nothing but commandlets that form an essential component of PowerShell. Cmdlets are lightweight commands written in .NET languages like C# or directly in PowerShell, and they follow a clear Verb-Noun naming convention. This means that when you see a command such as **`Get-Process`**, it tells you exactly that it retrieves information about processes, while **`Stop-Service`** indicates that it stops a service.

Cmdlets operate on objects rather than plain text. When you run a cmdlet, you get an output of objects that have properties and methods. This object-oriented approach allows you to easily filter, sort, and transform data. For example, you can pipe the output of **`Get-Process`** into **`Sort-Object`** to organize the data based on a specific property like CPU usage.

Another key feature is the modular nature of cmdlets. Rather than loading an entire library of commands, PowerShell loads only the cmdlets you need. This helps to keep your sessions fast and responsive. As you continue learning, you will also explore how cmdlets come with useful parameters such as **`-ErrorAction`** and **`-Verbose`** that allow you to control how errors are handled and to see detailed information about what each command is doing. The integrated IntelliSense in PowerShell 7.3 assists you with real-time suggestions and helps ensure that your syntax is correct, making your learning process both interactive and engaging.

Let us now explore some of the most popular cmdlets that you will encounter as you progress through your PowerShell journey. Below is a list of 25 commonly used cmdlets with practical examples to help you understand their usage:

Get-Process

This retrieves information about running processes. For example:

```
Get-Process | Sort-Object CPU -Descending | Select-Object -
First 5
```

This command sorts processes by CPU usage and displays the top five.

Get-Service

This one retrieves the status of services.

```
Get-Service | Where-Object { $_.Status -eq "Running" }
```

It filters the list to show only services that are running.

Get-ChildItem

It lists files and directories in a specified path.

```
Get-ChildItem -Path "C:\Windows" -Force
```

The **-Force** parameter includes hidden items.

Get-ItemProperty

This one retrieves the properties of a specified item, such as file attributes.

```
Get-ItemProperty -Path "C:\Windows\System32\cmd.exe"
```

It displays detailed properties of the item.

Set-Location

It changes your current working directory.

```
Set-Location -Path "C:\Windows\System32"
```

This command navigates you to the specified directory.

New-Item

It creates a new item, like a file or folder.

```
New-Item -Path "C:\temp\newfile.txt" -ItemType "File"
```

Remove-Item

It simply deletes a file or folder.

```
Remove-Item -Path "C:\temp\oldfile.txt" -Force
```

The **-Force** parameter ensures that even read-only files are deleted.

Rename-Item

Renames a file or directory.

```
Rename-Item -Path "C:\temp\file.txt" -NewName "newfile.txt"
```

It updates the file name to a new one.

Start-Process

This one launches a new process or application. For example:

```
Start-Process -FilePath "notepad.exe"
```

This command opens Notepad.

Stop-Process

This command terminates a running process by name or ID. For example:

```
Stop-Process -Name "notepad"
```

It stops all instances of Notepad.

Get-Content

It simply reads the contents of a file.

```
Get-Content -Path "C:\temp\file.txt"
```

By running the above command, it displays the text content of the file.

Set-Content

This one specifically writes or replaces content in a file.

```
Set-Content -Path "C:\temp\file.txt" -Value "Hello, PowerShell
7.3!"
```

It updates the file with the specified string.

Out-File

It sends output to a file instead of the console.

```
Get-ChildItem -Path "C:\temp" | Out-File -FilePath
"C:\temp\dirlist.txt"
```

Running this command will save the directory listing to a text file.

Get-Date

This one displays the current date and time.

```
Get-Date
```

This command returns the system's current date and time.

Get-Host

It retrieves information about your PowerShell host environment.

```
Get-Host
```

It shows details such as the version and UI culture.

Get-Module

This one lists the modules currently loaded in your session.

```
Get-Module -ListAvailable
```

It displays all available modules that you can import.

Import-Module

This command loads the module into your current session to add new functionality.

```
Import-Module -Name ActiveDirectory
```

It makes Active Directory cmdlets available for your use.

Export-CSV

This one helps to export object data to a CSV file for analysis or reporting.

```
Get-Process | Export-CSV -Path "C:\temp\processes.csv" -
NoTypeInformation
```

It exports process details without type metadata.

Test-Connection

This one pings a remote host to test network connectivity.

```
Test-Connection -ComputerName "google.com" -Count 4
```

It sends four ping requests and shows the results.

New-ADUser

Rthis is used to create a new user account in Active Directory.

```
New-ADUser -Name "John Doe" -GivenName "John" -Surname "Doe" `
  -UserPrincipalName "johndoe@contoso.com" `
  -AccountPassword (ConvertTo-SecureString "P@ssw0rd1" -
AsPlainText -Force)
```

It sets up a new Active Directory user with a secure password.

Get-ADUser

It simply retrieves details about an Active Directory user.

```
Get-ADUser -Identity "johndoe"
```

It generally fetches properties and account status for the user.

Set-ADUser

This one modifies properties of an existing Active Directory user.

```
Set-ADUser -Identity "johndoe" -Department "IT"
```

It updates the department attribute for the user.

Get-ADComputer

This quickly retrieves information about a computer object from Active Directory.

```
Get-ADComputer -Identity "computer1"
```

Here, it displays details about the computer's configuration and status.

Enable-ADAccount

Thia one enables a disabled user or computer account in Active Directory.

```
Enable-ADAccount -Identity "johndoe"
```

Doing this, it reactivates the specified account.

Disable-ADAccount

This one disables an active user or computer account in Active Directory.

```
Disable-ADAccount -Identity "johndoe"
```

It locks the account to prevent further actions.

As you go through these examples and practice using these cmdlets, you will build a solid base in PowerShell that will help you automate tasks and manage systems more effectively. The helpful tips you get when you need them, along with the ability to explore each command's settings and uses, makes learning a lot easier and more fun.

PowerShell Aliases

PowerShell aliases serve as alternative names for cmdlets, functions, and scripts. Aliases simplify your command line experience by reducing the amount of typing required for commonly used commands. When you work with aliases, you are not changing the underlying functionality; you are simply creating shorthand versions of longer commands. It makes your workflow more efficient and helps you focus on the task at hand.

Creating Aliases

When you create an alias, you use the **Set-Alias** cmdlet. For instance, instead of typing **Get-ChildItem** every time you list directory contents, you can define an alias such as **ls**:

```
Set-Alias -Name ls -Value Get-ChildItem
```

This simple command allows you to use **ls** as a quick shortcut. As you practice, you will find that aliases not only speed up your work but also make your command lines cleaner and easier to remember.

Modifying Aliases

You might sometimes need to change an existing alias. Using **Set-Alias** again, you can modify an alias to point to a different cmdlet. For example, if you decide that **ls** should reference **Get-**

Item instead, simply run:

```
Set-Alias -Name ls -Value Get-Item
```

If an alias no longer serves your purpose, you can remove it with **Remove-Item**. To remove the alias **ls**, type:

```
Remove-Item alias:ls
```

While these aliases simplify repetitive commands, overuse or ambiguous naming may lead to confusion, especially when sharing scripts with others.

PowerShell Functions

Let us now move on to PowerShell functions. It is a very powerful way to create reusable blocks of code. The functions allow you to encapsulate complex tasks into a single command that can accept input parameters, process data, and return output. It simplifies your scripts and also enhances modularity and reusability across your projects.

Defining a Simple Function

To define a function in PowerShell, you use the **function** keyword followed by the function name and a code block enclosed in curly braces. Think of a simple function that adds two numbers as below:

```
function Add-Numbers {
    param($num1, $num2)
    $sum = $num1 + $num2
    Write-Output "The sum of $num1 and $num2 is: $sum"
}
```

When you run **Add-Numbers -num1 10 -num2 15**, the function calculates and displays the result. This example shows how functions make repetitive tasks simpler.

Working with Parameters

Now the functions become even more powerful when you incorporate parameters. The parameters allow you to pass values into your function, making it flexible and adaptable. You can also define default values for parameters.

For example:

```
function Get-ProcessInfo {
    param(
        [string]$name = "notepad"
    )
    Get-Process -Name $name
}
```

In this case, if you do not specify a process name, the function defaults to retrieving information about **notepad**. This feature is particularly useful when you want to offer a standard behavior with the option to customize.

Advanced Function Features

As you grow more comfortable with functions, you will explore advanced features such as parameter validation, error handling, and pipeline input. For instance, you can enforce valid input using attributes like **[ValidateSet()]**:

```
function Set-ServiceStatus {
    [CmdletBinding()]
    param(
        [Parameter(Mandatory=$true)]
        [string]$service,
        [ValidateSet("Running", "Stopped")]
        [string]$status
    )
    Set-Service -Name $service -Status $status
}
```

Here, the **Set-ServiceStatus** command only accepts "Running" or "Stopped" as valid statuses, thereby preventing errors and ensuring correct usage. The **try-catch** blocks in your functions allows you to handle errors:

```
function Get-ProcessInfo {
    [CmdletBinding()]
    param(
```

```
        [Parameter(Mandatory=$true)]
        [string]$name
    )
    try {
        Get-Process -Name $name -ErrorAction Stop
    }
    catch {
        Write-Warning "Process '$name' not found."
    }
}
```

This function now warns you if the process is not found. One of the key benefits of functions is that they enable you to break down complex tasks into manageable parts. By writing functions for specific operations, you can reuse them across different scripts and projects. This modularity saves time, reduces errors, and makes your code easier to maintain.

Summary

To sum it up, we learned a lot in this chapter. You learned that cmdlets are the core building blocks of PowerShell and that they follow a clear Verb-Noun naming convention to perform specific tasks efficiently. You also saw how these lightweight commands worked on objects, letting you filter, sort, and transform data easily through pipelines. You also learned about the modular nature of cmdlets, which keeps your sessions fast by loading only the necessary commands. You practiced popular cmdlets that handle daily admin tasks, like process management, file operations, and Active Directory tasks.

Then, we tried out creating, modifying, and removing aliases, which helped make command execution more streamlined and reduced the amount of typing we had to do. You also learned how to create reusable functions that encapsulated specific logic, how to work with parameters including setting default values and validating input, and how to integrate advanced features such as error handling and pipeline input. All of this made you more confident and helped establish a solid foundation for automating routine tasks with PowerShell.

Chapter 4: Up and Running with Scripting Basics

Chapter Overview

This chapter will teach you the basics of PowerShell scripting and get you started on the automation aspects of PowerShell. It provides an overview of how to define and work with variables, and it teaches you the nuances of variable scope so that you can effectively manage data in different parts of your scripts. You'll learn about the different data types and operators, which are key for doing math and logical operations. You'll explore to write conditional statements and loops, so you can control the flow of your scripts based on dynamic conditions.

A good chunk of this chapter is all about mastering the PowerShell pipeline and output formatting, which are tools that let you chain commands and present data in a way that's easy to read. You'll learn by doing hands-on exercises with practical examples, so you can build a solid scripting base that sets the stage for more advanced techniques in future chapters. By the time you're done with this chapter, you'll have the key skills to write clear, efficient, and reliable scripts that automate routine tasks, making your system management more streamlined and effective.

Variables

Variables serve as named storage locations for data, which you can manipulate and use throughout your scripts. They provide a flexible way to store strings, numbers, arrays, objects, and more. In PowerShell, you create a variable by using the dollar sign ($) followed by the variable name. This method allows you to assign values and then reference those values later in your commands or scripts.

Creating Variables

When you create a variable, you assign a value using the equals sign (=). For example, if you type:

```
$name = "John Doe"

$age = 30
```

you create two variables: one that holds a string and another that holds an integer. You can access these values simply by referencing the variable names:

```
Write-Host "Name: $name"

Write-Host "Age: $age"
```

This outputs the values stored in the variables, allowing you to use them in any part of your script. You also learn that variables are case-insensitive in PowerShell, meaning that $name, $Name, and $NAME refer to the same variable. As you work with variables, you notice that they help you streamline your scripts, letting you store results from commands and reuse data without hardcoding values.

Data Types

Variables in PowerShell support a range of data types such as strings, integers, floats, booleans, arrays, and hashtables. You can create strings by enclosing text in single or double quotes, and you create arrays by listing items separated by commas, enclosed in parentheses.

For example:

```
$colors = @("Red", "Green", "Blue")
```

This creates an array that holds multiple color values. You will witness that the PowerShell automatically detects the data type based on the value assigned in order to work with different types of information without explicit type declarations.

Variable Scope

Variable scope defines where a variable is accessible within your PowerShell scripts. As you write more complex scripts, understanding scope becomes essential for controlling how and where variables are used. PowerShell supports several scopes, including global, local, script, and private, each serving a distinct purpose.

Global Scope

Global variables are accessible from anywhere in your session or any script that your current script runs. This means that if you declare a global variable, you can access it from functions, scripts, and even nested script blocks. To create a global variable, you use the prefix **$global:**. For example:

```
$global:companyName = "Contoso"
```

Here, the variable **companyName** is available globally throughout your session, ensuring that every part of your script can reference the company name.

Local Scope

Local variables are confined to the current scope, such as within a function or a script block. You simply declare these variables with the dollar sign ($), and they are only available in that specific context. If you declare a variable inside a function, it will not be accessible outside of that function.

Following is a quick example:

```
function Show-LocalVariable {
```

```
    $local:message = "This is a local variable"
    Write-Host $message
}
```

Here, the variable **message** is limited to the function **Show-LocalVariable**, preventing unintended interference with variables elsewhere in your script.

Script Scope

Script variables are accessible throughout the entire script in which they are declared, including within any functions or nested script blocks. You can define a script variable by using the prefix **$script:**.

For example:

```
$script:configFile = "C:\config\settings.xml"
```

Here, the variable is accessible anywhere within the script file, making it useful for storing configuration settings or other data that needs to be shared across different parts of the script.

Private Scope

Private variables are designed to be accessible only within the specific scope where they are declared and are not visible to child scopes. This can be useful when you need to ensure that a variable does not get inadvertently modified by functions or nested blocks. You create a private variable by using the prefix **$private:**.

For example:

```
$private:secret = "SensitiveData123"
```

The variable **secret** remains isolated within the current scope, protecting its value from external changes and ensuring that your sensitive data stays secure.

As you develop your PowerShell scripts, you will understand that the global variables simplify the process when data needs to be shared widely, while local and private variables help you avoid conflicts and accidental changes. Whereas, the script variables offer a balanced approach by being accessible throughout the script while still keeping the variable contained within that file.

Data Types

The data types in PowerShell is a key concept to work with various kinds of information. The data types include strings, integers, floats, booleans, arrays, and hashtables. Each type is used to represent different forms of data, and PowerShell automatically interprets the type based on the value you assign.

Working with Strings and Numbers

When you create a string, you enclose text in single or double quotes. For example, you can assign a message like this:

```
$greeting = "Welcome to PowerShell scripting!"
```

This variable now holds a string value. Similarly, you work with numbers by directly assigning them to variables. For instance:

```
$age = 25
```

The PowerShell distinguishes between integers and floating-point numbers, so you can assign a decimal value with a period:

```
$price = 19.99
```

This automatic detection makes it easier for you to focus on logic without worrying about explicit type declarations.

Arrays and Hashtables

Arrays allow you to store multiple items in a single variable. You create an array by listing elements separated by commas inside the **`@()`** syntax:

```
$colors = @("Red", "Green", "Blue")
```

You then access individual elements using their index. Hashtables, on the other hand, store key-value pairs. You define a hashtable with the **`@{}`** syntax:

```
$person = @{
    Name = "Alice"
    Age  = 30
    City = "Seattle"
}
```

This structure lets you retrieve values by referencing the corresponding key, such as **`$person["Name"]`**.

These data types are capable of determining how you manipulate and transform data. They affect operations like comparisons and arithmetic, and they also play a critical role when working with objects returned by cmdlets. The versatility of PowerShell's data types allows you to handle everything from simple text processing to complex data structures effortlessly.

Conditional Statements and Loops

The conditional statements and loops are the fundamental constructs to control the flow of your scripts. They let you execute code based on conditions and repeat actions such that the scripts turn dynamic and responsive to different inputs.

Conditional Statements

Conditional statements let you run specific code blocks when certain conditions are met. The primary statement is the **`if`** statement. For example, you might write:

```
$temperature = 75
if ($temperature -gt 80) {
    Write-Host "It's hot outside."
} elseif ($temperature -lt 60) {
    Write-Host "It's chilly outside."
} else {
    Write-Host "The temperature is moderate."
}
```

Here, the PowerShell evaluates each condition in order and executes the corresponding code block when the condition is true. You also have the **`switch`** statement, which simplifies checking a variable against multiple values:

```
$day = "Wednesday"
switch ($day) {
    "Monday" { Write-Host "Start of the work week." }
    "Friday" { Write-Host "End of the work week." }
    default  { Write-Host "Midweek day." }
}
```

This method is particularly useful when you have multiple specific values to compare.

Looping Constructs

Loops let you execute a block of code repeatedly. There are several types of loops in PowerShell, each with its own use case:

For Loop

The **for** loop is ideal when you know how many times you want to iterate. For example:

```
for ($i = 1; $i -le 5; $i++) {
    Write-Host "Iteration $i"
}
```

This loop runs exactly five times.

Foreach Loop

When you want to process each item in a collection, the **foreach** loop is your friend. For instance, with an array:

```
$names = @("Alice", "Bob", "Charlie")
foreach ($name in $names) {
    Write-Host "Hello, $name!"
}
```

Each element in the array is processed one by one.

While Loop

The **while** loop continues as long as a condition remains true. Consider:

```
$count = 1
while ($count -le 3) {
    Write-Host "Count is $count"
    $count++
}
```

This loop keeps running until the count exceeds 3.

Do-While Loop

A **do-while** loop ensures that the code block executes at least once, as it checks the condition after execution:

```
$counter = 1
do {
    Write-Host "Counter is $counter"
    $counter++
} while ($counter -le 3)
```

This guarantees that you always see at least one iteration.

As you write scripts, combining conditional statements with loops becomes a part of your day to day tasks. You might use an **if** statement inside a loop to decide whether to process an item or skip it, or employ a **switch** statement to handle multiple scenarios within iterative tasks.

PowerShell Pipeline

Let us now explore the PowerShell pipeline. It is a powerful feature that lets you pass the output of one command directly as input to another command. This mechanism enables you to build complex operations by linking simple, modular commands together. These pipeline transforms your workflow by eliminating the need to store intermediate results. The data flows seamlessly from one cmdlet to the next.

When you use the pipeline, the output of one cmdlet becomes an object or a set of objects that the next cmdlet in the chain processes. For example, you can retrieve a list of running processes with **Get-Process**, filter them using **Where-Object**, and format the results with **Format-Table** all in one continuous command:

```
Get-Process | Where-Object { $_.CPU -gt 100 } | Format-Table -
AutoSize
```

In this example, each process that meets the CPU usage condition flows directly into the table formatter, allowing you to see a neatly organized display of high-CPU processes. As you practice, you notice that the pipeline empowers you to combine the strengths of multiple cmdlets without writing intermediary variables.

Output Formatting

The next step is to focus on output formatting, an integral part of presenting data in PowerShell. When you run commands, the raw output can be a bit tricky to read or interpret. PowerShell has a bunch of cmdlets that let you tweak how the info is displayed, so you can get a clear, structured view of your data.

Formatting with Format-Table

The **Format-Table** cmdlet organizes your output into a neat table where each column represents a property of the objects being processed. As you work with **Format-Table**, you can use the **-AutoSize** parameter to automatically adjust column widths based on the content:

```
Get-Process | Format-Table -Property Name, CPU, ID -AutoSize
```

This command formats the process information into a table with columns for Name, CPU usage, and Process ID, ensuring that each column is sized appropriately for its content.

Using Format-List

When you need more detailed output, the **Format-List** cmdlet displays each object's properties on separate lines. This is particularly useful when objects have many properties or when values are long:

```
Get-Service | Where-Object { $_.Status -eq "Running" } |
Format-List -Property Name, DisplayName, Status
```

Here, the **Format-List** shows each service's properties in a clear, list-based format, making it easier to read detailed information.

Format-Wide and Format-Custom

For simpler outputs, **Format-Wide** displays a single property across the console, often in multiple columns:

```
Get-ChildItem | Format-Wide -Property Name -Column 3
```

This command shows only the names of files and folders, arranged in three columns for quick scanning.

For more tailored views, **Format-Custom** allows you to define your own layout using a script block:

```
Get-Process | Format-Custom -Property Name, CPU, ID -
Expression {

    "Process: " + $_.Name

    "CPU: " + $_.CPU
```

```
    "ID: " + $_.ID
    "---------------------"
}
```

The example creates a custom display that adds descriptive text to each property, providing a personalized output format.

As you integrate these formatting tools into your workflow, you find that the clarity and presentation of your data improve dramatically. Whether you are generating reports, debugging scripts, or simply reviewing command outputs, these formatting cmdlets help you transform raw data into insightful information.

Summary

In conclusion, the lessons in this chapter have been thorough and have provided you with a solid foundation in the basic scripting features of PowerShell. You got the hang of creating and using variables, and you understand how they store data and make it easier to manage dynamic information in your scripts. You learned about the different variable scopes—global, local, script, and private—and how each scope determines where a variable can be accessed in your scripts.

You discovered different data types, like strings, numbers, arrays, and hashtables, which let you work with all kinds of information easily. You got into conditional statements and loops, which let you control the flow of your scripts with if, switch, for, foreach, while, and do-while constructs. You also got a handle on the PowerShell pipeline, which lets you pass output from one command as input to another, creating efficient chains of commands. And finally, you learned how to format your script outputs so they're more readable and usable.

CHAPTER 5: WORKING WITH POWERSHELL MODULES

Chapter Overview

This chapter will give you the basics of PowerShell modules, which are key to creating reusable and maintainable code in your automation scripts. You'll learn how to organize your functions, cmdlets, and other resources into modules that can be easily imported and shared across multiple projects. We'll go through the whole process of creating a module from scratch, including how to structure your module folder, write a module file ***(.psm1)***, and generate a module manifest (.psd1) to provide metadata like version, author, and exported functions.

Next, you'll dive into the best practices for modularizing your code, which not only makes it more readable but also boosts collaboration and maintenance. We'll also show you some practical examples of how to build custom modules that extend PowerShell's functionality and how to import and use these modules in your sessions. By the time you're done with this chapter, you'll have the know-how to create, manage, and deploy your own modules, that will largely benefit you to streamline your scripting process and encourage code reuse.

Importing and Exporting Modules

Modules are packages that bundle together reusable code—such as cmdlets, functions, scripts, and additional resources—to help you manage and organize your PowerShell environment more efficiently. When you work with modules, you gain the ability to import functionality into your session, share code across scripts, and even distribute custom solutions. In PowerShell, modules are typically composed of a script module file ***(.psm1)***, a module manifest (.psd1) that contains metadata like the author, version, and dependencies, and sometimes a formatting file (.ps1xml) for customized output. Modules allow you to extend the native capabilities of PowerShell, making your automation tasks more streamlined and manageable. You can work with built-in modules provided by Microsoft or create your own custom modules to encapsulate the functions and logic that you frequently use. This simplifies code maintenance, and also fosters a reusable environment that accelerates your scripting efforts.

Importing Modules

When you want to use the functionality contained within a module, you begin by importing it into your PowerShell session using the **Import-Module** cmdlet. For example, if you have a module file named **MyGreetingModule.psm1** saved in a known directory, you can import it like this:

```
Import-Module -Name "C:\path\to\MyGreetingModule.psm1"
```

Once imported, all the functions and cmdlets defined in that module become available for you to use in your current session. Therefore, you can call a function such as **Get-Greeting**—defined in your module—without having to include its code every time you run a script.

Exporting Modules

When you create a module, you've got to think about more than just writing your functions. You also have to decide which parts of your module you're going to expose. You control this with the **Export-ModuleMember** cmdlet inside your module file. For instance, after defining a function like **Get-Greeting** in **MyGreetingModule.psm1**, you add the following line at the end of your file:

```
Export-ModuleMember -Function Get-Greeting
```

This command ensures that only the **Get-Greeting** function is exported and made accessible when the module is imported. It is useful when you want to hide internal helper functions that should not be exposed to users.

Creating and Managing Custom Modules

To create your own custom module, you need to begin with writing the functions you need in a PowerShell script file and save it with a ***.psm1*** extension. Next, create a module manifest using the **New-ModuleManifest** cmdlet to define metadata such as the author, version, and list of exported commands. Then, just save both files in one of the directories listed in the **$env:PSModulePath** environment variable, or specify a custom path when importing.

Now, if you want to discover which modules are available on your system, which can be done by using:

```
Get-Module -ListAvailable
```

For any additional functionality in your system, you may simply install modules from the PowerShell Gallery using **Install-Module**. To keep your modules up to date, use the **Update-Module** cmdlet.

Creating Custom Modules

Custom modules allow you to encapsulate functions, variables, and even entire scripts into a single, manageable file that you can import into any session. This process not only saves you time by avoiding repeated code but also helps you maintain a clean and organized scripting environment.

Writing Module Functions

The first step in creating a custom module is to write the functions and scripts you want to include. For example, think of a simple function that returns a greeting message:

```
function Get-Greeting {
    param (
        [string]$Name = "User"
    )
    "Hello, $Name! Welcome to your custom module."
}
```

As you type, you notice that the function follows the Verb-Noun naming convention, which makes its purpose clear.

Once you have a set of functions ready, save your code in a file with the ***.psm1*** extension. For instance, you could save the above function in a file named **MyGreetingModule.psm1**. This file represents your module, and all functions written within will be part of it. Storing your module in a consistent location (such as a directory listed in the **$env:PSModulePath** environment variable) makes it easier for PowerShell to locate and import your module later.

Creating a Module Manifest

While a simple ***.psm1*** file can function as a module, creating a module manifest is a best practice that adds structure and metadata to your module. For this, use the **New-ModuleManifest** cmdlet to generate a manifest file with the **.psd1** extension. The manifest includes important details like the module version, author, description, and a list of functions to export.

To do this, run the following command in your PowerShell session:

```
New-ModuleManifest -Path
"C:\Modules\MyGreetingModule\MyGreetingModule.psd1" -
RootModule "MyGreetingModule.psm1" -Author "Your Name" -
Description "A custom module that provides greeting
functions." -ModuleVersion "1.0"
```

This command creates a manifest that ties together your script module and provides valuable information for anyone using or maintaining the module.

Importing and Exporting Functions

Within your ***.psm1*** file, after writing all your functions, add an **Export-ModuleMember** statement to specify which functions should be available when someone imports your module. For xample, the below line:

```
Export-ModuleMember -Function Get-Greeting
```

tells PowerShell that when you import **MyGreetingModule.psm1**, only the **Get-Greeting** function should be accessible.

Now over the time, you might include multiple functions, variables, and even nested modules. So this needs how better you organize your code into logical sections with clear comments. For example, group related functions together, and consider using regions or headers in your code to separate different parts. This makes the module easier to read and maintain.

Testing Custom Module

Before using your module in production, you must test it thoroughly. Open a new PowerShell session and import your module using:

```
Import-Module -Name
"C:\Modules\MyGreetingModule\MyGreetingModule.psm1"
```

After importing, call the functions to ensure they behave as expected:

```
Get-Greeting -Name "John"
```

If the output matches your expectations, your module is working correctly. Otherwise, review the code, check the manifest, and make necessary adjustments. Testing helps you catch errors early and ensures that the module integrates seamlessly with other scripts.

If you follow these steps, you can build a custom module that holds your PowerShell functions, making your scripts more modular, easy to maintain, and reusable. In the long run, this practice will not only save you time, but it will also allow you to share powerful functionality across projects and team environments.

Summary

To recap, the lessons in this chapter focused on understanding and working with PowerShell modules. You learned that modules are basically packages of reusable code, like cmdlets, functions, and scripts. These help you organize and share functionality across sessions. You learned how to import a module into your session using Import-Module and how to export specific functions with Export-ModuleMember to control what's made available.

Later, you gained some hands-on experience by creating a custom module, writing functions, and saving them in a **.psm1** file. Then, you enhanced it with a module manifest to provide metadata and manage exports. You also learned how to test your module by importing it into a new session and calling its functions, as well as how to modify and update your module as your requirements changed. tutorials to see how modules can simplify script management, promote code reuse, and maintain organization in your PowerShell projects.

Chapter 6: PowerShell Scripting

Chapter Overview

This chapter will teach you how to script in PowerShell, from the basics to making your own automated workflows. You'll learn how to plan and write scripts that effectively manage system tasks, making your day-to-day operations more efficient. We'll focus on how to structure your scripts, use clear and meaningful variable names, and implement advanced error handling with try-catch blocks to gracefully manage exceptions. You'll also dive into incorporating logging mechanisms that record script execution details, so you've got a comprehensive audit trail for troubleshooting and performance monitoring.

The chapter will also cover running scripts in different situations, like interactive sessions and automated batch processes, so you can choose the best approach for various scenarios. You'll see practical, hands-on examples of how to create scripts that perform multi-step operations—ranging from file management to service control—while ensuring consistency and reliability. By the time you finish this chapter, you'll have the skills needed to automate repetitive tasks. Plus, you'll lay the groundwork for more advanced automation strategies that we'll cover in the next chapters.

Writing and Executing Scripts

Imagine you need to automate the organization of files in a specified folder. Your goal is to monitor a folder, detect new files, and move them to subfolders based on their file extension. This scenario probvides you a ready script I prepared long time back, that helps you manage cluttered directories efficiently. You will work with advanced scripting constructs without revisiting basic variable or loop teachings from earlier chapters.

Planning and Structure

At first, before writing any code, you try to outline the script's workflow:

- Monitor a specific folder for new files.
- Check each file's extension to determine its category (e.g., .txt, .jpg, .pdf).
- Move the file to a corresponding subfolder.
- Handle errors gracefully if the file is in use or the destination folder does not exist.

Script Implementation

Now, look at the following example script of a robust file organizer. It employs advanced error handling and control structures to ensure smooth execution:

```
# Define the source directory and destination mapping
```

```
$sourceFolder = "C:\FilesToOrganize"
$destinationMap = @{
    ".txt" = "C:\FilesToOrganize\TextFiles"
    ".jpg" = "C:\FilesToOrganize\Images"
    ".pdf" = "C:\FilesToOrganize\PDFs"
}
# Ensure destination directories exist
foreach ($extension in $destinationMap.Keys) {
    $destPath = $destinationMap[$extension]
    if (-not (Test-Path -Path $destPath)) {
        try {
            New-Item -Path $destPath -ItemType Directory -
ErrorAction Stop
            Write-Host "Created directory: $destPath"
        }
        catch {
            Write-Warning "Failed to create directory
$destPath: $_"
        }
    }
}
# Process each file in the source folder
Get-ChildItem -Path $sourceFolder -File | ForEach-Object {
    $file = $_
    $fileExtension = $file.Extension.ToLower()
    if ($destinationMap.ContainsKey($fileExtension)) {
        $destination = $destinationMap[$fileExtension]
        try {
            # Attempt to move the file
```

```
            Move-Item -Path $file.FullName -Destination
$destination -ErrorAction Stop
            Write-Host "Moved '$($file.Name)' to
'$destination'"
        }
        catch {
            Write-Warning "Error moving '$($file.Name)': $_"
        }
    }
    else {
        Write-Host "No designated folder for extension
$fileExtension. Skipping '$($file.Name)'."
    }
}
```

Here, we start by defining the source folder and a mapping between file extensions and their corresponding destination directories. The script will check if each destination directory exists; if not, it attempts to create it with robust error handling. Next, it then retrieves all files from the source folder, processes each file by checking its extension, and moves it accordingly. The **try-catch** blocks ensure that if an error occurs (for example, if a file is locked), the script logs a warning rather than halting execution entirely.

Now, to execute this script, we need to save it with a **.ps1** extension (e.g., **FileOrganizer.ps1**), for which we need to first open the PowerShell session, and run:

```
.\FileOrganizer.ps1
```

After this, you have a complete, advanced script that automates a common administrative task.

Modify Existing Script

Now, let us try to modify an existing PowerShell script by building upon the file organizer script we previously implemented. To do this, it involves identifying areas for improvement, applying changes, and then testing the modifications to ensure everything works as intended.

Identifying Modification Requirements

So let us begin. Here, we will consider that we want to extend the file organizer script to include logging functionality. In addition to moving files based on their extension, you want to record every successful move and any errors encountered during execution. This log can be invaluable for troubleshooting and auditing script performance. Your task is to modify the existing script so that it writes detailed entries to a log file, such as **organizer.log**, every time a file is moved or an error occurs.

Implementing Changes

Now to implement the changes, we need to determine where to insert the logging mechanism in your script. You can define a new variable for the log file path at the top of the script:

```
$logFile = "C:\FilesToOrganize\organizer.log"
```

Next, create a helper function to write log entries with a timestamp. For example:

```
function Write-Log {
    param(
        [string]$Message
    )
    $timestamp = Get-Date -Format "yyyy-MM-dd HH:mm:ss"
    $logEntry = "$timestamp - $Message"
    Add-Content -Path $logFile -Value $logEntry
}
```

Now, integrate calls to this helper function into your existing logic. For instance, after successfully moving a file, call **Write-Log** to record the action:

```
try {
    Move-Item -Path $file.FullName -Destination $destination -
ErrorAction Stop
    Write-Host "Moved '$($file.Name)' to '$destination'"
    Write-Log "Moved '$($file.Name)' to '$destination'"
}
catch {
    Write-Warning "Error moving '$($file.Name)': $_"
    Write-Log "Error moving '$($file.Name)': $_"
```

```
}
```

This integration logs both successful moves and errors. Ensure that the log file variable is defined before you begin processing the files.

Testing Modified Script

Once you have made your modifications, save the updated script (e.g., **FileOrganizer.ps1**) and run it in your PowerShell session. Check the log file specified by **$logFile** to verify that entries are being recorded as expected.

This whole simple practice demonstrates how you can take an existing script and extend its functionality without starting from scratch.

PowerShell Parameters

PowerShell parameters let you write flexible scripts that accept inputs from users, other scripts, or automated processes. You can define parameters in your script to enable different use cases without hardcoding values or modifying your script's internal logic. You can also specify mandatory parameters, default values, parameter validation, and multiple parameter sets to deal with complex scenarios.

Defining Parameters

When you write a PowerShell script, you declare parameters using a **param** block at the top of the file. This block contains one or more parameters, each with a name, optional attributes, and possibly a default value.

Given below is a simple example:

```
param(
    [Parameter(Mandatory=$true)]
    [string]$Path,
    [Parameter(Mandatory=$false)]
    [int]$MaxSize = 100
)
```

It defines two parameters:

- **Path**, which is mandatory and must be specified by the user, and

- **MaxSize**, which is optional and defaults to 100 if the user does not provide a value.

Mandatory, Optional, and Default Values

A mandatory parameter forces the user or calling process to provide an argument. If the user omits a mandatory parameter, PowerShell displays an error and stops execution. This behavior prevents scripts from running with incomplete data. Optional parameters, on the other hand, allow a script to run with sensible defaults or user-provided values, increasing flexibility.

The following example illustrates both:

```
param(
    [Parameter(Mandatory=$true)]
    [string]$SourceFolder,
    [Parameter(Mandatory=$false)]
    [string]$DestinationFolder = "C:\Backup"
)
```

Here, the **SourceFolder** must be specified, while **DestinationFolder** defaults to **C:\Backup** if the user does not specify a path.

Parameter Validation

Advanced scripts often include parameter validation to ensure that inputs meet certain criteria. You can use built-in attributes such as **[ValidateRange()]**, **[ValidatePattern()]**, **[ValidateSet()]**, or **[ValidateScript()]** to enforce rules on user inputs. Here is an example of **[ValidateRange()]** and **[ValidatePattern()]**:

```
param(
    [Parameter(Mandatory=$true)]
    [ValidatePattern("^([A-Za-z]:\\).+")]
    [string]$FolderPath,
    [Parameter(Mandatory=$true)]
    [ValidateRange(1, 100)]
    [int]$RetentionDays
)
```

In the above,

- **[ValidatePattern("^([A-Za-z]:\).+")]** ensures that **FolderPath** matches a basic pattern for a drive letter followed by a backslash and additional characters (a simple validation for a Windows path).
- **[ValidateRange(1, 100)]** requires that **RetentionDays** be between 1 and 100, inclusive.

If a user attempts to run the script with values outside these rules, PowerShell halts and displays an error.

Using Parameter Sets

Parameter sets enable you to create scripts that accept different combinations of parameters for different use cases. Each parameter set can define a unique subset of mandatory parameters, and PowerShell enforces these sets at runtime. It is helpful when you have a script that can operate in multiple modes.

Let us understand it better through the following simplified example:

```
param(
    [Parameter(Mandatory=$true, ParameterSetName="ByName")]
    [string]$UserName,
    [Parameter(Mandatory=$true, ParameterSetName="ById")]
    [int]$UserId
)
switch ($PSCmdlet.ParameterSetName) {
    "ByName" {
        Write-Host "Script running in ByName mode. UserName:
$UserName"
        # Additional logic for name-based processing
    }
    "ById" {
        Write-Host "Script running in ById mode. UserId:
$UserId"
        # Additional logic for ID-based processing
    }
}
```

Here, the script can run in **ByName** mode (requiring **UserName**) or **ById** mode (requiring **UserId**).

Pipeline Input

When writing advanced scripts, you may want to allow pipeline input. This capability means that your script can accept objects from another command, rather than relying on command-line arguments. You achieve this by decorating parameters with **[Parameter(ValueFromPipeline=$true)]** or **[Parameter(ValueFromPipelineByPropertyName=$true)]**.

Try the following example:

```
param(
    [Parameter(ValueFromPipeline=$true)]
    [string]$FileName
)
process {
    # For each incoming object, the FileName parameter is
automatically bound
    # if it matches the correct type or property name
    if (Test-Path $FileName) {
        Write-Host "File '$FileName' exists."
    } else {
        Write-Host "File '$FileName' does not exist."
    }
}
```

You can call the above script by piping a list of files:

```
"file1.txt","C:\Docs\report.pdf" | .\CheckFile.ps1
```

After calling, each object in the pipeline is passed to **CheckFile.ps1**, which tests its existence.

Sample Program: Automated Backup

A more detailed script that illustrates advanced parameter usage is so mthing I have created as below. It backs up files from one place to another, and it lets you choose how long you want to keep your files. You can also add extra steps to the process.

```
param(
    [Parameter(Mandatory=$true, ValueFromPipeline=$true)]
    [ValidatePattern("^([A-Za-z]:\\).+")]
    [string]$Source,
    [Parameter(Mandatory=$false)]
    [string]$Destination = "C:\DefaultBackup",
    [Parameter(Mandatory=$false)]
    [ValidateRange(1, 365)]
    [int]$RetentionDays = 30
)
process {
    # Ensure destination exists
    if (-not (Test-Path -Path $Destination)) {
        New-Item -ItemType Directory -Path $Destination | Out-
Null
    }
    # Copy all items from Source to Destination
    Write-Host "Backing up files from $Source to
$Destination..."
    try {
        Copy-Item -Path $Source\* -Destination $Destination -
Recurse -ErrorAction Stop
        Write-Host "Backup completed successfully."
    }
    catch {
        Write-Warning "Failed to back up files: $_"
        return
    }
    # Apply retention policy if requested
```

```
    Write-Host "Applying retention policy of $RetentionDays
days..."
    $cutoffDate = (Get-Date).AddDays(-$RetentionDays)
    Get-ChildItem -Path $Destination -Recurse | Where-Object {
        $_.LastWriteTime -lt $cutoffDate
    } | ForEach-Object {
        try {
            Remove-Item -Path $_.FullName -Recurse -
ErrorAction Stop
            Write-Host "Removed old file/folder: $($_.Name)"
        }
        catch {
            Write-Warning "Failed to remove old item: $_"
        }
    }
}
```

In the above script,

- The script requires a **Source** directory, validates it with a simple pattern, and allows the user to pass it through the pipeline or directly. The **Destination** parameter defaults to **C:\DefaultBackup**, and **RetentionDays** defaults to 30, ensuring a safe baseline configuration.
- The script checks if the destination directory exists and creates it if necessary.
- A **Copy-Item** operation copies all files from the source to the destination, with error handling to ensure any issues are logged via warnings rather than abrupt termination.
- The script calculates a cutoff date and removes files older than the specified number of days, providing feedback on each deletion attempt.

Now, to run this script with positional or named arguments, you could execute:

```
.\BackupScript.ps1 -Source "C:\Project" -Destination
"D:\Archive" -RetentionDays 60
```

Or you could simply pipeline multiple source paths if the script is designed to handle them:

```
"C:\Project1","C:\Project2" | .\BackupScript.ps1 -Destination
"D:\Archive"
```

After implementing parameters, test your script with a variety of inputs wherein you check that mandatory parameter prompt for values when omitted, that optional parameters default to expected values, and that validation attributes correctly block invalid data.

Using Parameters

A practical way to incorporate parameters into your file organizer script is to let users specify the source folder and an optional path for the log file, rather than hardcoding those values. It makes your script more flexible, since it can adapt to various environments without requiring changes to the internal code.

Below is a revised version of the file organizer script that adds parameters for the source folder and an optional log file path. Now in this, you must notice the **param** block at the top, which defines both parameters and enforces that the **SourceFolder** is mandatory:

```
param(
    [Parameter(Mandatory=$true)]
    [ValidatePattern("^([A-Za-z]:\\).+")]
    [string]$SourceFolder,
    [Parameter(Mandatory=$false)]
    [string]$LogFile = $null
)
# Define a helper function for logging
function Write-OrganizerLog {
    param(
        [string]$Message
    )
    if ($LogFile) {
        $timestamp = Get-Date -Format "yyyy-MM-dd HH:mm:ss"
        $logEntry = "$timestamp - $Message"
        Add-Content -Path $LogFile -Value $logEntry
```

```
    }
}
# Define a simple extension-to-folder map
$destinationMap = @{
    ".txt" = "$SourceFolder\TextFiles"
    ".jpg" = "$SourceFolder\Images"
    ".pdf" = "$SourceFolder\PDFs"
}
# Ensure destination directories exist
foreach ($extension in $destinationMap.Keys) {
    $destPath = $destinationMap[$extension]
    if (-not (Test-Path -Path $destPath)) {
        try {
            New-Item -Path $destPath -ItemType Directory -
ErrorAction Stop
            Write-Host "Created directory: $destPath"
            Write-OrganizerLog "Created directory: $destPath"
        }
        catch {
            Write-Warning "Failed to create directory
$destPath: $_"
            Write-OrganizerLog "Failed to create directory
$destPath: $_"
        }
    }
}
# Process each file in the source folder
Get-ChildItem -Path $SourceFolder -File | ForEach-Object {
    $file = $_
    $fileExtension = $file.Extension.ToLower()
```

```
    if ($destinationMap.ContainsKey($fileExtension)) {
        $destination = $destinationMap[$fileExtension]
        try {
            Move-Item -Path $file.FullName -Destination
$destination -ErrorAction Stop
            Write-Host "Moved '$($file.Name)' to
'$destination'"
            Write-OrganizerLog "Moved '$($file.Name)' to
'$destination'"
        }
        catch {
            Write-Warning "Error moving '$($file.Name)': $_"
            Write-OrganizerLog "Error moving '$($file.Name)':
$_"
        }
    }
    else {
        Write-Host "No designated folder for extension
$fileExtension. Skipping '$($file.Name)'."
        Write-OrganizerLog "Skipped '$($file.Name)' (no folder
for $fileExtension)."
    }
}
```

When you run this updated script, PowerShell prompts you for **SourceFolder** if it is not provided.

```
.\FileOrganizer.ps1 -SourceFolder "C:\FilesToOrganize" -
LogFile "C:\FilesToOrganize\organizer.log"
```

This command processes files in **C:\FilesToOrganize** and writes log entries to **organizer.log**.

Arguments and Argument Parsing

Arguments is very closely related to parameters but encompassing more practical ways of passing data into your scripts. Arguments can come from command-line input, environment variables, or even other scripts.

When you define parameters in a PowerShell script, you can accept arguments in two main ways: **`positional`** or **`named`**. Positional arguments rely on the order in which you pass them, whereas named arguments explicitly match parameter names to their values.

They are generally understood as

- **`Positional Arguments`**: If a parameter has a **`Position`** attribute set (for example, **`Position=0`**), you can pass its value without naming the parameter, as long as it is in the correct order.
- **`Named Arguments`**: Here, you specify the parameter name followed by a value, allowing you to pass arguments in any order. It improves clarity, especially in scripts with multiple parameters.

Sample Program: Multi-Mode Backup

To understand it better, let us consider that there is a backup script that can operate in two modes:

1. **`Local`**: Copies files from one local folder to another.
2. **`Remote`**: Copies files from a local folder to a remote network share.

You define parameters with different attributes and parameter sets, and then show how to call them with both positional and named arguments. Below is a script snippet demonstrating advanced argument parsing:

```
param(
    # This parameter set handles local backups
    [Parameter(Mandatory=$true, ParameterSetName="Local",
Position=0)]
    [string]$SourceLocal,
    [Parameter(Mandatory=$true, ParameterSetName="Local",
Position=1)]
    [string]$DestinationLocal,
    # This parameter set handles remote backups
    [Parameter(Mandatory=$true, ParameterSetName="Remote",
Position=0)]
```

```
    [string]$SourceRemote,
    [Parameter(Mandatory=$true, ParameterSetName="Remote",
Position=1)]
    [string]$RemoteShare,
    [Parameter(Mandatory=$false)]
    [switch]$VerboseMode
)
switch ($PSCmdlet.ParameterSetName) {
    "Local" {
        if ($VerboseMode) { Write-Host "Running in Local
mode..." }
        Copy-Item -Path $SourceLocal -Destination
$DestinationLocal -Recurse
        if ($VerboseMode) { Write-Host "Local backup completed
from $SourceLocal to $DestinationLocal." }
    }
    "Remote" {
        if ($VerboseMode) { Write-Host "Running in Remote
mode..." }
        Copy-Item -Path $SourceRemote -Destination
$RemoteShare -Recurse
        if ($VerboseMode) { Write-Host "Remote backup
completed from $SourceRemote to $RemoteShare." }
    }
}
```

In the above script, there are two **Parameter Sets**:

- Local requires SourceLocal and DestinationLocal.
- Remote requires SourceRemote and RemoteShare.
- Both sets define two parameters at positions 0 and 1.

This means you can call them positionally as **.\MultiBackup.ps1 C:\Data D:\Archive** for the Local set.

If you prefer clarity, you can name your arguments, e.g. .\MultiBackup.ps1 -SourceLocal "C:\Data" -DestinationLocal "D:\Archive".

By constructing your script with parameter sets, you guide PowerShell's argument parser to validate which parameters belong together. This stops invalid combinations and makes it easier for people using the script.

Parsing Arguments from Pipeline

In more advanced scenarios, you can allow pipeline input by specifying **`[Parameter(ValueFromPipeline=$true)]`** on parameters. This lets you pass objects from other cmdlets into your script:

```
param(
    [Parameter(Mandatory=$true, ValueFromPipeline=$true)]
    [string]$FilePath
)
process {
    if (Test-Path $FilePath) {
        Write-Host "File '$FilePath' found."
    } else {
        Write-Warning "File '$FilePath' not found."
    }
}
```

With this, you could run:

```
"file1.txt","file2.log" | .\FileCheck.ps1
```

and PowerShell automatically binds each string to the **`$FilePath`** parameter in turn, iterating through the **`process`** block for each incoming item.

Summary

So, to sum it up, the main thing we learned in this chapter was how to create more advanced PowerShell scripts that go beyond simple sequences of commands. You learned how to plan out your script, use techniques like error handling and try-catch blocks to prevent sudden failures, and more. You also explored a file organizer scenario that moved files based on extensions and showed how to integrate logging mechanisms without repeating earlier lessons.

Then, you learned how to modify an existing script by adding functionality, showing that scripts could evolve without requiring a complete rewrite. You also checked out how parameters can be defined in scripts to accept user input, including mandatory and optional parameters, default values, and validation attributes that enforce certain rules on the supplied data. You also looked at argument parsing in PowerShell, which let you handle positional and named arguments, switch between parameter sets, and even accept pipeline input. All of this shows how you can make flexible, easy-to-maintain scripts that can adapt to different situations in real life.

CHAPTER 7: WINDOWS MANAGEMENT WITH POWERSHELL

Chapter Overview

This chapter will walk you through the powerful features of Windows management with PowerShell. You'll learn how to interact with the file system like a pro, including advanced techniques for managing files, folders, and drives. You'll also learn how to automate and streamline your administrative tasks. You'll also dive into working with the Windows Registry, treating it like an accessible data store to configure and maintain system settings. As you go through it, you'll also learn about managing system processes, services, and event logs.

Next, you'll discover practical methods to monitor system performance, control service behavior, and troubleshoot issues through log analysis. The chapter will also cover managing scheduled tasks, teaching you how to automate routine operations, create maintenance schedules, and handle task modifications and removals. Upon completion of this chapter, you will have a well-rounded set of skills that will enable you to use PowerShell to manage and optimize Windows environments.

Managing Files, Folders, and Drives

PowerShell equips you with a comprehensive set of cmdlets to perform routine tasks—such as creating, moving, renaming, and deleting files and directories—while also allowing you to automate complex operations. You begin by learning to navigate through the file system. The **Set-Location** cmdlet (or its alias, cd) lets you change the current working directory. For instance, to switch to your Users folder, you type:

```
Set-Location -Path C:\Users
```

You can check your current directory with **Get-Location** (or pwd), which displays your present working directory.

Creating and Removing Directories

To create a new folder called "Example" in the C: drive, you use:

```
New-Item -Path "C:\Example" -ItemType Directory
```

If you later need to remove the "Example" folder, especially if it contains files or subdirectories, you rely on **Remove-Item** with the **-Recurse** switch:

```
Remove-Item -Path "C:\Example" -Recurse
```

These commands allow you to automate the setup or teardown of directory structures, an essential task in many administrative routines.

Creating, Reading, and Editing Files

Files form the core of many operations, and PowerShell provides robust support for file manipulation.

To create a new file, you use **New-Item** specifying the file type:

```
New-Item -Path "C:\Example\test.txt" -ItemType File
```

Once the file exists, you can read its contents with **Get-Content**:

```
Get-Content -Path "C:\Example\test.txt"
```

To write new data, **Set-Content** overwrites the file's content:

```
Set-Content -Path "C:\Example\test.txt" -Value "Hello, World!"
```

For appending additional lines without overwriting, **Add-Content** is ideal:

```
Add-Content -Path "C:\Example\test.txt" -Value "This is a new
line."
```

You may also need to replace specific text within a file. By combining **Get-Content**, **ForEach-Object**, and **Set-Content**, you can perform in-place replacements:

```
(Get-Content -Path "C:\Example\test.txt") |
ForEach-Object { $_ -replace "World", "PowerShell" } |
Set-Content -Path "C:\Example\test.txt"
```

This method lets you automate text updates across many files, saving you from manual edits.

Copying, Moving, and Renaming

PowerShell has a straightforward method to copy, move, and rename files or directories. For example, to copy a file, you use **Copy-Item**:

```
Copy-Item -Path "C:\Example\test.txt" -Destination
"C:\Example\test_copy.txt"
```

To move the file, **Move-Item** does the trick:

```
Move-Item -Path "C:\Example\test.txt" -Destination
"C:\Example\test_moved.txt"
```

If renaming is needed, **Rename-Item** allows you to change the file name:

```
Rename-Item -Path "C:\Example\test.txt" -NewName
"test_renamed.txt"
```

All these can be integrated into larger automation scripts to maintain orderly file systems.

Working with Drives

In addition to managing individual files and folders, you will also work with drives. The **Get-PSDrive** cmdlet lists all available drives, both logical and mapped network drives:

```
Get-PSDrive
```

Changing the current drive is as simple as using **Set-Location**:

```
Set-Location -Path "D:"
```

To obtain detailed information about a specific drive, **Get-Volume** provides insights such as free space and capacity:

```
Get-Volume -DriveLetter D
```

These commands help you monitor and manage your storage devices effectively.

Filtering, Sorting, and Attributes

PowerShell provides powerful filtering and sorting capabilities through cmdlets like **Get-ChildItem** and **Sort-Object**. You can list all text files in a directory by using:

```
Get-ChildItem -Path "C:\Example" -Filter "*.txt"
```

To recursively list files, include the **-Recurse** switch:

```
Get-ChildItem -Path "C:\Example" -Recurse
```

You may also sort files by a specific property, such as the last write time:

```
Get-ChildItem -Path "C:\Example" | Sort-Object -Property
LastWriteTime
```

The management of file and folder attributes is also straightforward. Say, to check a file's attributes, use:

```
(Get-Item -Path "C:\Example\test.txt").Attributes
```

To set an attribute—say, making a file read-only—use **Set-ItemProperty**:

```
Set-ItemProperty -Path "C:\Example\test.txt" -Name Attributes
-Value ([System.IO.FileAttributes]::ReadOnly)
```

To remove the read-only attribute, you can perform bitwise operations:

```
$attributes = (Get-Item -Path
"C:\Example\test.txt").Attributes
$attributes = $attributes -band (-bnot
[System.IO.FileAttributes]::ReadOnly)
Set-ItemProperty -Path "C:\Example\test.txt" -Name Attributes
-Value $attributes
```

Calculating Folder Size

An essential aspect of file management is determining the size of a folder. If you combining **Get-ChildItem** with **Measure-Object**, you can sum the sizes of all files within a folder:

```
$folderSize = (Get-ChildItem -Path "C:\Example" -Recurse -File
| Measure-Object -Property Length -Sum).Sum
Write-Host "Folder size: $($folderSize / 1MB) MB"
```

This command provides a quick overview of storage consumption for maintenance and planning. Whether you are setting up a new directory structure, automating file transfers, or cleaning up old files, these commands provide a powerful and flexible interface for file management tasks.

Working with Windows Registry

The Windows Registry is a critical component for system configuration and application settings. The Windows Registry is a hierarchical database that stores configuration data and settings for both the operating system and installed applications. PowerShell treats the registry as a navigable data store, similar to a file system, using special drives like **HKLM:** and **HKCU:** to represent the HKEY_LOCAL_MACHINE and HKEY_CURRENT_USER hives, respectively.

Navigating Registry

To begin, you use the **Set-Location** cmdlet to navigate the registry. For example, to access the SOFTWARE section under HKEY_LOCAL_MACHINE, you type:

```
Set-Location -Path "HKLM:\SOFTWARE"
```

You can view the current registry location with **Get-Location** and list registry keys using **Get-ChildItem**. It allows you to traverse the registry as if it were a standard directory structure.

Reading Registry Keys and Values

Once you have navigated to the desired hive, you can read registry keys and their values. The **Get-Item** cmdlet fetches a registry key, while **Get-ItemProperty** retrieves the values within that key. For example:

```
Get-Item -Path
"HKLM:\SOFTWARE\Microsoft\Windows\CurrentVersion"
```

To read a specific value, such as the directory where programs are installed, you use:

```
Get-ItemProperty -Path
"HKLM:\SOFTWARE\Microsoft\Windows\CurrentVersion" -Name
"ProgramFilesDir"
```

This command returns the value associated with the "ProgramFilesDir" property.

Creating and Removing Registry Keys

PowerShell allows you to create new registry keys using **New-Item**. To create a key under HKEY_CURRENT_USER, you might run:

```
New-Item -Path "HKCU:\Software\ExampleKey"
```

If a key is no longer needed, remove it with **Remove-Item**:

```
Remove-Item -Path "HKCU:\Software\ExampleKey"
```

These operations enable you to modify the registry structure directly from PowerShell, facilitating automated configuration changes.

Managing Registry Values

Beyond keys, you also manage registry values. You can use **Set-ItemProperty** to create or update a registry value. For instance, to set a value under a key you just created:

```
Set-ItemProperty -Path "HKCU:\Software\ExampleKey" -Name
"ExampleValue" -Value "PowerShell" -Type String
```

If you need to remove a specific value, use **Remove-ItemProperty**:

```
Remove-ItemProperty -Path "HKCU:\Software\ExampleKey" -Name
"ExampleValue"
```

These commands give you granular control over individual registry settings for fine-tuning system behavior.

Exporting and Importing Registry Keys

For backup or migration purposes, you may need to export parts of the registry. PowerShell simplifies this with the **Export-RegistryFile** cmdlet:

```
Export-RegistryFile -Path "HKCU:\Software\ExampleKey" -
Destination "C:\Example\ExampleKey.reg"
```

This command creates a .reg file that can later be imported using **Import-RegistryFile**:

```
Import-RegistryFile -Path "C:\Example\ExampleKey.reg"
```

These operations are particularly useful when deploying settings across multiple systems or recovering configurations after a system restore.

Searching Registry

Sometimes you need to find specific registry keys or values. You can perform a recursive search by combining **Get-ChildItem** with **Where-Object**. For example, to find keys that contain the word "Example":

```
Get-ChildItem -Path "HKLM:\SOFTWARE" -Recurse | Where-Object {
$_.Name -like "*Example*" }
```

It helps you quickly locate the registry entries you need to modify.

The ability to work with the registry through PowerShell is a powerful way to automate system configuration. For example, if you're in charge of setting up a software configuration on a bunch of machines, you can write a script that reads the current registry settings, makes changes as needed, and then exports the configuration for auditing. And if you script the backup of specific registry hives, you've got a recovery point before making big system changes.

Managing Processes, Services, and Event Logs

Managing Processes

Processes are active programs running on your system, and managing them efficiently is key to ensuring optimal performance. PowerShell provides robust cmdlets that let you query and control these processes.

Listing Processes

To retrieve a list of all running processes, you use the **Get-Process** cmdlet. For instance:

```
Get-Process
```

This command returns detailed information such as process names, IDs, CPU usage, and memory consumption. You can filter the results to focus on specific processes. For example, to display only processes that include "chrome" in their name:

```
Get-Process | Where-Object { $_.Name -like "*chrome*" }
```

Starting and Stopping Processes

When you need to launch an application, **Start-Process** is your go-to command. For example, to open Notepad:

```
Start-Process -FilePath "notepad.exe"
```

Conversely, if you need to terminate a process, **Stop-Process** is available. You can stop a process by its name or process ID:

```
Stop-Process -Name "notepad"
```

If we integrate these commands into our script, it will allow us to automate the management of processes, such as restarting a service or closing unresponsive applications.

Working with Services

Services are background processes that run without user interaction, playing a vital role in system operations. PowerShell provides a suite of cmdlets to monitor and control these services.

Listing and Filtering Services

To view all services, use the **Get-Service** cmdlet:

```
Get-Service
```

If you want to filter services by their status, such as listing only those that are running, you can pipe the output to **Where-Object**:

```
Get-Service | Where-Object { $_.Status -eq "Running" }
```

Controlling Services

To start a service, the **Start-Service** cmdlet is used. For example, to start the Windows Update service:

```
Start-Service -Name "wuauserv"
```

Similarly, you can stop a service with **Stop-Service**:

```
Stop-Service -Name "wuauserv"
```

Here, changing a service's startup type is also possible using **Set-Service**:

```
Set-Service -Name "wuauserv" -StartupType "Manual"
```

These commands enable you to automate service management to make sure that the necessary services are running and unnecessary ones are halted.

Monitoring and Managing Event Logs

Event logs are the system's audit trail, capturing important events, warnings, and errors that occur within the Windows environment. PowerShell allows you to interact with these logs to monitor system health and diagnose issues.

Viewing Event Logs

To list all available event logs, you use the **Get-EventLog** cmdlet with the **-List** parameter:

```
Get-EventLog -List
```

This command displays a list of logs, such as Application, System, and Security, along with details about their sizes and number of entries.

Reading Specific Logs

To inspect the content of a log, such as the Application log, you run:

```
Get-EventLog -LogName Application -Newest 20
```

This command retrieves the 20 most recent entries, allowing you to quickly scan for issues.

Filtering and Searching

You can narrow down the log entries using filters. For example, to display only error events from the Application log, you type:

```
Get-EventLog -LogName Application | Where-Object {
$_.EntryType -eq 'Error' }
```

Similarly, to search for events related to a specific source:

```
Get-EventLog -LogName Application | Where-Object { $_.Source -
eq 'MyApp' }
```

Exporting and Clearing Logs

For audit or backup purposes, you may need to export logs. To export the Application log to a CSV file:

```
Get-EventLog -LogName Application -Newest 100 | Export-Csv -
Path "C:\Logs\ApplicationLog.csv" -NoTypeInformation
```

If required, you can clear an event log using:

```
Clear-EventLog -LogName Application
```

These techniques allow you to maintain, archive, or reset logs as part of your regular system maintenance routines.

Sample Program: A Health Check Script

Imagine you are tasked with writing a health check script for a server. The script must:

- List all running processes, highlighting any that use excessive CPU.
- Check the status of critical services and start them if they are stopped.
- Retrieve recent error events from the Application log and export them for review.

The given below is a sample program that integrates these tasks:

```
# Health Check Script
```

```
# Check for high CPU processes (CPU usage above 80)
$highCpuProcesses = Get-Process | Where-Object { $_.CPU -gt 80
}
if ($highCpuProcesses) {
    Write-Host "High CPU usage detected:"
    $highCpuProcesses | Format-Table Name, CPU, ID -AutoSize
} else {
    Write-Host "No processes exceeding CPU usage threshold."
}
# Check critical service status (example: Windows Update
service)
$service = Get-Service -Name "wuauserv"
if ($service.Status -ne "Running") {
    Write-Host "Service 'wuauserv' is not running. Attempting
to start..."
    Start-Service -Name "wuauserv"
    Write-Host "'wuauserv' started successfully."
} else {
    Write-Host "Service 'wuauserv' is running."
}
# Retrieve recent error events and export them
$recentErrors = Get-EventLog -LogName Application -Newest 50 |
Where-Object { $_.EntryType -eq 'Error' }
if ($recentErrors) {
    $exportPath = "C:\Logs\RecentErrors.csv"
    $recentErrors | Export-Csv -Path $exportPath -
NoTypeInformation
    Write-Host "Exported recent error events to $exportPath"
} else {
    Write-Host "No recent error events found in the
Application log."
```

```
}
```

This above program provides a detailed health check, combining process monitoring, service management, and event log analysis.

Managing Scheduled Tasks

Scheduled Tasks are essential for automating routine operations such as system maintenance, backups, and data processing. PowerShell provides a suite of cmdlets that allow you to create, modify, run, and delete scheduled tasks such that we can have full control over automation without needing to interact with the graphical Task Scheduler interface.

Listing and Retrieving Tasks

To begin with it, you first start by learning how to list all scheduled tasks on your system. The **Get-ScheduledTask** cmdlet is the primary tool for this:

```
Get-ScheduledTask
```

This command retrieves a list of tasks, displaying their names, status, and other pertinent details. To retrieve information about a specific task, you can filter by task name:

```
Get-ScheduledTask -TaskName "MyScheduledTask"
```

This command provides detailed information, that can contribute for monitoring and troubleshooting tasks.

Creating New Scheduled Tasks

Creating a new scheduled task involves defining an action, a trigger, and then registering the task. Consider a scenario where you want to run a script daily at 6:00 AM. Follow these steps:

Define Action

Use **New-ScheduledTaskAction** to specify the executable or script to run. For instance, to run a PowerShell script located at **C:\Scripts\DailyBackup.ps1**, you use:

```
$action = New-ScheduledTaskAction -Execute "PowerShell.exe" -
Argument "-File C:\Scripts\DailyBackup.ps1"
```

Define Trigger

Create a trigger that specifies when the task should run. For a daily task at 6:00 AM, use:

```
$trigger = New-ScheduledTaskTrigger -Daily -At 6am
```

Register Task

With the action and trigger defined, register the task using **Register-ScheduledTask**:

```
Register-ScheduledTask -TaskName "DailyBackup" -Action $action
-Trigger $trigger -Description "Daily backup script."
```

This process creates a new scheduled task that will run your backup script every day at the specified time.

Modifying Existing Scheduled Tasks

You may need to update a scheduled task to change its trigger or action. Begin by retrieving the task:

```
$task = Get-ScheduledTask -TaskName "DailyBackup"
```

Once retrieved, update the desired properties. For instance, if you need to change the scheduled time, create a new trigger:

```
$newTrigger = New-ScheduledTaskTrigger -Daily -At 7am
```

Then, apply the changes with **Set-ScheduledTask**:

```
Set-ScheduledTask -TaskName "DailyBackup" -Trigger $newTrigger
```

This command updates the task's trigger, ensuring that the backup script now runs at 7:00 AM instead of 6:00 AM.

Running and Stopping Scheduled Tasks

Sometimes you need to manually run or stop a scheduled task for testing or maintenance purposes. To run a task manually, use **Start-ScheduledTask**:

```
Start-ScheduledTask -TaskName "DailyBackup"
```

If you need to stop a running task, **Stop-ScheduledTask** is available:

```
Stop-ScheduledTask -TaskName "DailyBackup"
```

These commands give you immediate control over task execution, which is especially useful during troubleshooting or script testing.

Enabling, Disabling, and Removing Tasks

Managing the state of scheduled tasks is critical for system maintenance. To disable a task, which prevents it from running until you are ready, use **Disable-ScheduledTask**:

```
Disable-ScheduledTask -TaskName "DailyBackup"
```

Conversely, to enable it again, use **Enable-ScheduledTask**:

```
Enable-ScheduledTask -TaskName "DailyBackup"
```

If a task is no longer needed, remove it completely with **Unregister-ScheduledTask**:

```
Unregister-ScheduledTask -TaskName "DailyBackup" -
Confirm:$false
```

This command deletes the task without prompting for confirmation, ensuring a clean removal.

Sample Program: Holistic Maintenance Task

Let's say you need to do weekly system maintenance. This maintenance includes running a cleanup script, checking for disk errors, and generating a report. You can set up a scheduled task to run this maintenance script every Sunday at midnight. The script could include detailed logging and error handling, similar to the file organizer example.

Following is an example of how you could set this up:

First, we develop a PowerShell script (**Maintenance.ps1**) that performs the necessary cleanup and diagnostics. And, then we set up the action to run the script with PowerShell:

```
$maintenanceAction = New-ScheduledTaskAction -Execute
"PowerShell.exe" -Argument "-File C:\Scripts\Maintenance.ps1 -
Verbose"
```

Next, we create a trigger for weekly execution:

```
$maintenanceTrigger = New-ScheduledTaskTrigger -Weekly -
DaysOfWeek Sunday -At "12:00 AM"
```

Finally, we register the maintenance task:

```
Register-ScheduledTask -TaskName "WeeklyMaintenance" -Action
$maintenanceAction -Trigger $maintenanceTrigger -Description
"Performs weekly system maintenance."
```

This whole setup ensures that your maintenance tasks are automated and run consistently without manual intervention. In practice, you can monitor the task's execution and adjust the schedule as needed, using the techniques outlined above.

Summary

Overall, the stuff we learned in this chapter gave us a solid overview of Windows management using PowerShell. You got the hang of file system operations, like navigating, creating, modifying, and deleting files and folders. You also explored some advanced techniques for managing drives, filtering items, and calculating folder sizes. You also learned how to interact with the Windows Registry, from navigating its structure to reading, modifying, exporting, and importing keys and values.

The chapter also went into more detail about managing system processes and services, giving you methods to list, control, and monitor their status. You also covered techniques for filtering and analyzing event logs, which are essential for troubleshooting and system health checks. Finally, you learned how to manage scheduled tasks, including how to create, modify, and control task execution, which lets you automate recurring administrative tasks effectively. All of these topics together gave you the tools to keep the Windows environment in check, monitor it, and find ways to make it better using PowerShell.

CHAPTER 8: ACTIVE DIRECTORY MANAGEMENT

Chapter Overview

This chapter is going to take you on a deeper dive into Active Directory management using PowerShell. You'll learn how to use the Active Directory PowerShell module to do all sorts of admin tasks, like creating and managing user accounts, groups, and computers, and organizing all that within Organizational Units. The chapter will walk you through the steps of setting up configurations, tweaking attributes, and automating repetitive tasks in Active Directory. This helps keep your infrastructure consistent and secure. You'll also learn how to deal with complex scenarios like moving computer accounts, enforcing group policies, and integrating with other systems for centralized management.

By using the learnings and the techniques explored, you'll be able to streamline Active Directory administration and reduce the risks associated with manual configuration errors. When you are finished with this chapter, you will be equipped with automation tools and strategies to help you maintain the scalable, well-organized, and secure Active Directory environment.

Active Directory PowerShell Module

Active Directory PowerShell module is a powerful tool that enables you to manage Active Directory Domain Services (AD DS) and Active Directory Lightweight Directory Services (AD LDS) directly from PowerShell. This module bundles together a range of cmdlets that let you perform everyday administrative tasks with ease. Whether you need to manage user accounts, groups, computers, or organizational units (OUs), the AD module provides a consistent and efficient way to interact with Active Directory objects.

Discovering Module's Structure and Cmdlets

The AD PowerShell module follows the standard verb-noun naming convention that PowerShell users appreciate. For instance, cmdlets like **`Get-ADUser`**, **`Get-ADGroup`**, and **`Get-ADComputer`** allow you to retrieve information about different objects in Active Directory. This consistency in naming helps to remember the purpose of each cmdlet and discover new ones using the **`Get-Command -Module ActiveDirectory`** command.

When you run:

```
Get-Command -Module ActiveDirectory
```

The PowerShell returns a list of all available AD cmdlets, providing you with a clear map of the module's capabilities. Each cmdlet is designed to perform a specific operation—for example, **`New-ADUser`** creates a new user account, while **`Remove-ADUser`** deletes an existing account. You quickly see how these commands can be combined to build powerful scripts for bulk operations, such as creating multiple users or updating group memberships in one go.

Managing Users, Groups, and Computers

One of the module's core strengths is its ability to manage users. With **New-ADUser**, you can create user accounts with detailed properties like names, email addresses, and group affiliations. To understand better, try the following example:

```
New-ADUser -Name "John Doe" -GivenName "John" -Surname "Doe" `

-SamAccountName "jdoe" -UserPrincipalName
"jdoe@yourdomain.com" `

-AccountPassword (ConvertTo-SecureString "P@ssw0rd" -
AsPlainText -Force) `

-Enabled $true
```

Here, the command demonstrates how to create a new user, specifying critical details while ensuring that the account is enabled immediately. You also learn how to modify user attributes using **Set-ADUser**—for example, updating a user's title or department as your organization evolves.

Similarly, managing groups becomes a streamlined process. With cmdlets like **New-ADGroup**, **Get-ADGroup**, and **Add-ADGroupMember**, you can create groups, retrieve group details, and manage memberships effectively. For instance, adding a user to a group is as simple as:

```
Add-ADGroupMember -Identity "IT Support" -Members "jdoe"
```

For computer objects, the AD module provides **New-ADComputer**, **Get-ADComputer**, and **Set-ADComputer**. These commands allow you to create new computer accounts, retrieve detailed information, and update properties such as the description or location. When you combine these cmdlets with the ability to filter and sort data, you gain significant control over your domain's resources.

Organizing with Organizational Units

Another key aspect of the AD module is its support for managing Organizational Units. OUs allow you to logically group objects like users, groups, and computers for easier management and delegation of administrative tasks. With **New-ADOrganizationalUnit**, you can create new OUs, and with **Get-ADOrganizationalUnit** and **Set-ADOrganizationalUnit**, you can retrieve and modify their properties. These cmdlets help you maintain a well-organized Active Directory structure for effective delegation and policy enforcement.

For example, to create a new OU within your domain, you might use:

```
New-ADOrganizationalUnit -Name "Sales" -Path
"DC=yourdomain,DC=com"
```

This command creates an OU specifically for the Sales department, allowing you to apply targeted group policies and delegate administrative control to the appropriate personnel.

Advanced Features and Scripting Integration

Beyond basic management, the AD module integrates smoothly into larger PowerShell scripts that automate complex tasks. You learn how to incorporate AD cmdlets into scripts that perform bulk operations, such as migrating users from one OU to another or resetting passwords for multiple accounts. These scripts often include error handling with try-catch blocks to ensure that any issues are logged and managed without interrupting the overall process.

For example, a bulk user update script might look like this:

```
$users = Get-ADUser -Filter * -SearchBase
"OU=Sales,DC=yourdomain,DC=com"

foreach ($user in $users) {

    try {

        Set-ADUser -Identity $user -Title "Sales Associate"

        Write-Host "Updated $($user.SamAccountName)
successfully."

    }

    catch {

        Write-Warning "Failed to update
$($user.SamAccountName): $_"

    }

}
```

This snippet shows how you can iterate over a collection of user objects and apply changes conditionally, ensuring that your AD remains current and reflective of organizational changes.

The module's consistency, coupled with its robust error handling and security features, makes it an indispensable tool for any Active Directory administrator looking to streamline daily operations.

Installing Active Directory Module

Now, we move on to the installation process for the Active Directory module, as it is a prerequisite for managing AD objects using PowerShell. If done, it allows you to access a rich set of cmdlets designed for managing user accounts, groups, computers, and organizational units in your Active Directory environment.

Installing on Windows Server

On Windows Server, the Active Directory module is available as part of the Remote Server Administration Tools (RSAT) package. To install the module on a Windows Server, you typically use the **`Install-WindowsFeature`** cmdlet. This command installs the RSAT-AD-PowerShell feature, which includes all necessary cmdlets for Active Directory management.

For example, to install the Active Directory module on Windows Server, open an elevated PowerShell session and run:

```
Install-WindowsFeature -Name RSAT-AD-PowerShell
```

This command initiates the installation process. PowerShell will then download and install the required components, making the module available for use. After the installation is complete, you can verify the installation by importing the module:

```
Import-Module ActiveDirectory
```

To confirm that the module is loaded, list its cmdlets:

```
Get-Command -Module ActiveDirectory
```

This series of commands confirms that the Active Directory module is installed and ready to use on your Windows Server.

Installing on Windows

For client operating systems like Windows 10 or Windows 11, the Active Directory module is not installed by default. Instead, you install it through the RSAT package. Microsoft provides RSAT as an optional feature that can be added via the Settings app or through PowerShell.

To install the Active Directory module on Windows 10/11 using PowerShell, execute the following command:

```
Add-WindowsCapability -Online -Name Rsat.ActiveDirectory.DS-
LDS.Tools~~~~0.0.1.0
```

This command downloads and installs the RSAT Active Directory tools, including the Active Directory module. Once the installation is complete, you need to import the module to start using it:

```
Import-Module ActiveDirectory
```

Again, verify the installation by listing the available AD cmdlets:

```
Get-Command -Module ActiveDirectory
```

Now here, we have seen that even with a straightforward installation process, you may encounter issues. Here are some common problems and their solutions:

- Module Not Found

If you run **Import-Module ActiveDirectory** and receive an error that the module is not found, verify that RSAT is installed correctly. On client machines, ensure that the RSAT Active Directory DS-LDS Tools capability is present by running:

```
Get-WindowsCapability -Online | Where-Object Name -like
"Rsat.ActiveDirectory*"
```

If the state is not "Installed," re-run the installation command.

- Permission Errors

Sometimes, running AD cmdlets requires elevated permissions. Always run PowerShell as an administrator, particularly when modifying Active Directory objects.

- Network Connectivity Issues

In a domain environment, ensure that your machine is properly connected to the network and can communicate with domain controllers. DNS issues or network misconfigurations can lead to problems when executing AD cmdlets.

Once the module is installed and verified, you can begin leveraging its capabilities in your scripts and daily tasks. For example, you might automate routine tasks such as user provisioning, group management, or computer account cleanup.

Manage AD Users

Now we move onto managing the Active Directory users using the AD PowerShell module. Here, we will learn to create, modify, retrieve, and remove user accounts such that it helps to handle bulk operations or individual modifications without any concerns.

Creating New User Accounts

When you need to add a new user to Active Directory, the **New-ADUser** cmdlet becomes your primary tool. This command allows you to set multiple attributes at once. For example, to create a new user account for "John Doe," you might execute:

```
New-ADUser -Name "John Doe" `
    -GivenName "John" `
    -Surname "Doe" `
    -SamAccountName "jdoe" `
    -UserPrincipalName "jdoe@yourdomain.com" `
    -AccountPassword (ConvertTo-SecureString "P@ssw0rd" -
AsPlainText -Force) `
    -Enabled $true `
    -Path "OU=Users,DC=yourdomain,DC=com"
```

This command sets up the user's full name, login name, principal name, password, and the OU where the account should reside.

Retrieving User Information

To get details about a specific user, use **Get-ADUser**. This cmdlet retrieves user properties that are essential for reporting or further modifications. For instance:

```
Get-ADUser -Identity "jdoe" -Properties *
```

This command returns all properties of the user "jdoe." You can also filter users by criteria such as department or job title. For example, to list all users in the Sales department:

```
Get-ADUser -Filter { Department -eq "Sales" } -Properties
Department
```

The filters in the **Get-ADUser** helps you quickly gather specific information without retrieving unnecessary data.

Modifying User Attributes

After creating user accounts, you may need to update their information as roles change or additional details become available. The **Set-ADUser** cmdlet is used for this purpose. To update a user's title, for instance, you might run:

```
Set-ADUser -Identity "jdoe" -Title "IT Support Specialist"
```

This command directly updates the title attribute of the "jdoe" account. You can also modify multiple attributes simultaneously. For example, to change both the department and office location:

```
Set-ADUser -Identity "jdoe" -Department "IT" -Office "Building A, Room 101"
```

Such commands enable you to keep user information current and accurate.

Resetting Passwords and Account Control

The security aspect is also a must in Active Directory management. When a user forgets their password or a security breach is suspected, you might need to reset the password. You can use **`Set-ADAccountPassword`** to achieve this:

```
Set-ADAccountPassword -Identity "jdoe" -NewPassword
(ConvertTo-SecureString "NewP@ssw0rd" -AsPlainText -Force)
```

After resetting a password, you can also enable or disable an account with **`Enable-ADAccount`** or **`Disable-ADAccount`**. For example, to disable an account temporarily:

```
Disable-ADAccount -Identity "jdoe"
```

And to re-enable it:

```
Enable-ADAccount -Identity "jdoe"
```

These commands ensure that user accounts are properly controlled according to organizational policies.

Removing User Accounts

When a user leaves the organization or no longer requires access, you can remove their account using **`Remove-ADUser`**. For instance:

```
Remove-ADUser -Identity "jdoe" -Confirm:$false
```

This command deletes the "jdoe" account without prompting for confirmation. Always use caution when removing accounts, as this action cannot be easily undone.

Bulk Operations and Scripting Integration

In many environments, you need to manage multiple users at once. By leveraging PowerShell's ability to work with arrays and pipeline input, you can automate bulk operations. For example, suppose you have a CSV file containing new user data. You can import the CSV and create user accounts with a loop:

```
Import-Csv -Path "C:\NewUsers.csv" | ForEach-Object {
    New-ADUser -Name $_.Name `
        -GivenName $_.GivenName `
        -Surname $_.Surname `
        -SamAccountName $_.SamAccountName `
        -UserPrincipalName $_.UserPrincipalName `
        -AccountPassword (ConvertTo-SecureString $_.Password -
AsPlainText -Force) `
        -Enabled $true `
        -Path $_.OU
}
```

This script automates user creation, ensuring consistency and reducing manual errors. Similarly, you can update or disable users in bulk by filtering user objects with **Get-ADUser** and piping the results to **Set-ADUser** or **Disable-ADAccount**.

Manage AD Groups

The management of groups in Active Directory is vital for organizing users and controlling access to resources. Tasks like to create, retrieve, modify, and remove groups, as well as manage group memberships need to be skilled using the Active Directory PowerShell module. These tasks form the backbone of effective access control and resource management in an enterprise setting.

Creating New Groups

To create a new group, you use the **New-ADGroup** cmdlet. This cmdlet allows you to specify various properties, such as the group's name, scope, and category. For example, to create a global security group for the IT Support department, you might execute:

```
New-ADGroup -Name "IT Support" `
    -GroupScope Global `
    -GroupCategory Security `
    -Path "OU=Groups,DC=yourdomain,DC=com"
```

This command sets up a new group named "IT Support" within a specified OU, which can later be used to control access to IT resources. The **GroupScope** and **GroupCategory** parameters define the group's characteristics and its role within the domain.

Retrieving Group Information

Once groups are created, you often need to retrieve their details. The **Get-ADGroup** cmdlet helps you fetch information about specific groups. For instance:

```
Get-ADGroup -Identity "IT Support" -Properties *
```

This command retrieves all properties for the "IT Support" group, allowing you to review its settings and membership. To list all groups in a specific OU, you can use a filter:

```
Get-ADGroup -Filter * -SearchBase
"OU=Groups,DC=yourdomain,DC=com"
```

Such commands are particularly useful for audits and generating reports on group configurations.

Modifying Group Attributes

Active Directory groups may need to be updated as organizational needs change. You can modify group properties using the **Set-ADGroup** cmdlet. For example, if you need to change the description of a group, execute:

```
Set-ADGroup -Identity "IT Support" -Description "Group for IT
support personnel"
```

This command updates the description, providing clearer context for the group's purpose. You might also update other attributes such as the display name or group scope, depending on your requirements.

Managing Group Memberships

One of the most common tasks in group management is adding or removing members. The **Add-ADGroupMember** and **Remove-ADGroupMember** cmdlets streamline these operations. To add a user to the "IT Support" group:

```
Add-ADGroupMember -Identity "IT Support" -Members "jdoe"
```

Similarly, to remove a user from the group:

```
Remove-ADGroupMember -Identity "IT Support" -Members "jdoe" -
Confirm:$false
```

For bulk operations, you can simply pipe a list of users from a CSV file into these cmdlets, such that it automates the process of updating group memberships across the organization.

Removing Groups

When a group is no longer needed, you can remove it using **Remove-ADGroup**. For example:

```
Remove-ADGroup -Identity "IT Support" -Confirm:$false
```

This command deletes the group without prompting for confirmation, which is useful for scripted cleanup operations.

Automating Bulk Group Operations

For environments with many groups, you may need to perform bulk operations. Suppose you have a list of groups in a CSV file and you want to update their descriptions. You can use the following script:

```
Import-Csv -Path "C:\GroupUpdates.csv" | ForEach-Object {
    Set-ADGroup -Identity $_.GroupName -Description
$_.Description
    Write-Host "Updated group: $($_.GroupName)"
}
```

This script imports the CSV file, iterates through each record, and updates the corresponding group description. Bulk operations like this reduce manual effort and ensure consistency across your domain.

Manage Computer

Managing computer objects efficiently is essential for maintaining an organized network environment, enforcing security policies, and ensuring that software deployment and configuration are performed consistently across the organization. So here, we now put focus on managing computer accounts within Active Directory using the AD PowerShell module.

Creating Computer Accounts

To add a new computer account to Active Directory, you can simply use the **New-ADComputer** cmdlet. This command allows you to specify essential properties such as the computer's name, account name, and the organizational unit (OU) in which it should reside. For example, to create a new computer account named "Computer01" in the "Computers" OU, you can run:

```
New-ADComputer -Name "Computer01" -SamAccountName "Computer01"
-Path "OU=Computers,DC=example,DC=com"
```

This command sets up the computer account with a unique identifier and places it in the designated OU.

Retrieving Computer Information

Next, once the computer accounts are created, you often need to retrieve details about them. The **Get-ADComputer** cmdlet allows you to pull information about a specific computer or list multiple computers based on filters. For instance, to retrieve all properties of "Computer01", use:

```
Get-ADComputer -Identity "Computer01" -Properties *
```

This command provides comprehensive details, such as the computer's distinguished name, operating system version, and last logon time. You can also filter computers based on criteria, for example, listing all computers within a particular OU:

```
Get-ADComputer -Filter * -SearchBase
"OU=Computers,DC=example,DC=com"
```

Modifying Computer Account Properties

Modifying computer accounts is a common task, whether you need to update the computer description, change its location, or modify other attributes. The **Set-ADComputer** cmdlet is used for this purpose. For example, if you want to update the description of "Computer01" to indicate it is a test machine, you would execute:

```
Set-ADComputer -Identity "Computer01" -Description "This is a
test computer"
```

This command updates the computer's properties in Active Directory. You might also need to update other attributes such as the operating system details or physical location. As you experiment, consider using **Get-ADComputer** to retrieve the current settings, make your changes, and then verify them with another retrieval command.

Moving Computer Accounts Between OUs

Organizational changes may require moving a computer account from one OU to another. The **Move-ADObject** cmdlet is designed for such operations. First, retrieve the computer account object:

```
$computer = Get-ADComputer -Identity "Computer01"
```

Then, move the object to a new OU:

```
Move-ADObject -Identity $computer -TargetPath
"OU=NewComputers,DC=example,DC=com"
```

This command relocates the computer account, ensuring that it adheres to new organizational structures.

Disabling and Enabling Computer Accounts

For security or maintenance reasons, you might need to temporarily disable a computer account. The **Disable-ADAccount** cmdlet serves this purpose.

For example, to disable "Computer01":

```
Disable-ADAccount -Identity "Computer01"
```

Later, when the computer should be reactivated, use **Enable-ADAccount**:

```
Enable-ADAccount -Identity "Computer01"
```

These commands are particularly useful in scenarios where a computer is decommissioned, undergoing maintenance, or needs to be isolated for security audits.

Removing Computer Accounts

When a computer is no longer part of your environment, you must remove its account to maintain a clean Active Directory. The **Remove-ADComputer** cmdlet deletes the computer object from AD. For example:

```
Remove-ADComputer -Identity "Computer01" -Confirm:$false
```

This command deletes "Computer01" without prompting for confirmation. You can use this cmdlet with caution, as removal is irreversible unless you have backups or a robust recovery strategy in place.

Automating Bulk Computer Management

In larger environments, you may need to manage computer accounts in bulk. For instance, if you have a CSV file with a list of computer names and new descriptions, you can use:

```
Import-Csv -Path "C:\ComputerUpdates.csv" | ForEach-Object {
```

```
    Set-ADComputer -Identity $_.ComputerName -Description
$_.Description
    Write-Host "Updated computer: $($_.ComputerName)"
}
```

This script automates the update process for each computer in the CSV, ensuring consistency and saving significant time compared to manual updates.

Manage Organizational Units

OUs are key for organizing users, groups, computers, and other objects in your domain. You can delegate administrative control, apply group policies, and maintain a logical structure in your directory by effectively managing OUs.

Creating Organizational Units

To begin organizing your Active Directory, you can create new OUs using the **New-ADOrganizationalUnit** cmdlet. For example, to create an OU named "Sales" within your domain, you run:

```
New-ADOrganizationalUnit -Name "Sales" -Path
"DC=yourdomain,DC=com"
```

This command sets up an OU specifically for the Sales department, providing a dedicated space to manage user and computer accounts related to that division.

Retrieving and Viewing OU Information

Once OUs are created, you can view their details using the **Get-ADOrganizationalUnit** cmdlet. To retrieve all properties of a specific OU, for example, the "Sales" OU, use:

```
Get-ADOrganizationalUnit -Identity
"OU=Sales,DC=yourdomain,DC=com"
```

This command displays comprehensive information, including the OU's distinguished name and any associated properties. To list all OUs in your domain, you can run:

```
Get-ADOrganizationalUnit -Filter *
```

Modifying OU Attributes

Over time, you may need to update the properties of an OU. Whether it's a change in description, location, or other metadata, the **Set-ADOrganizationalUnit** cmdlet allows you to modify these attributes. For example, to update the description of the "Sales" OU:

```
Set-ADOrganizationalUnit -Identity
"OU=Sales,DC=yourdomain,DC=com" -Description "Sales Department
and Support"
```

This command updates the description, making it clearer for administrators and automated systems what the OU represents.

Renaming and Moving OUs

Organizational changes might require you to rename or move OUs. To rename an OU, use the **Rename-ADObject** cmdlet. For example, if you need to rename "Sales" to "Sales & Marketing," run:

```
Rename-ADObject -Identity "OU=Sales,DC=yourdomain,DC=com" -
NewName "Sales & Marketing"
```

This updates the OU's name while preserving its existing properties and membership.

To move an OU to a different location within the directory, use the **Move-ADObject** cmdlet. Suppose you want to move the renamed OU under a different parent OU; you can do so by:

```
Move-ADObject -Identity "OU=Sales &
Marketing,DC=yourdomain,DC=com" -TargetPath
"OU=Departments,DC=yourdomain,DC=com"
```

Removing Organizational Units

When an OU is no longer required, you can remove it using the **Remove-ADOrganizationalUnit** cmdlet. For instance, to delete an OU named "ObsoleteOU" without confirmation, run:

```
Remove-ADOrganizationalUnit -Identity
"OU=ObsoleteOU,DC=yourdomain,DC=com" -Confirm:$false
```

Be cautious when removing OUs, as this action permanently deletes all objects contained within, unless they are moved beforehand.

Automating Bulk OU Management

In environments with a large number of OUs, you might need to perform bulk operations. For example, if you have a CSV file listing new OU names and their parent paths, you can import the CSV and create multiple OUs in one go:

```
Import-Csv -Path "C:\OUList.csv" | ForEach-Object {
    New-ADOrganizationalUnit -Name $_.Name -Path $_.ParentPath
    Write-Host "Created OU: $($_.Name) in $($_.ParentPath)"
}
```

Similarly, you can update or move multiple OUs by processing a CSV file or using appropriate filters.

Manage Group Policy Objects (GPOs)

Let us now explore how to manage GPOs. We know that they are essential for enforcing settings and configurations on users and computers within an Active Directory environment. We can automate the creation, modification, linking, and removal of GPOs using PowerShell.

Importing Group Policy Module

Before working with GPOs, you need to import the Group Policy module. This module contains cmdlets specifically designed for Group Policy management. To do this, run:

```
Import-Module GroupPolicy
```

This command loads the necessary cmdlets, allowing you to interact with GPOs directly. You can verify the module's availability by listing its commands:

```
Get-Command -Module GroupPolicy
```

Creating New GPOs

One of the primary tasks in Group Policy management is creating new GPOs to apply configurations to users or computers. To create a new GPO, use the **New-GPO** cmdlet. For instance, if you want to create a GPO named "SecuritySettings" for enforcing password policies and account lockout policies, run:

```
New-GPO -Name "SecuritySettings"
```

This command creates a new GPO in the Group Policy Management Console (GPMC) with the specified name. Once created, you can further customize it by modifying its settings.

Retrieving GPO Information

After creating a GPO, it is often necessary to review its settings or confirm its creation. The **Get-GPO** cmdlet retrieves detailed information about a specific GPO. For example:

```
Get-GPO -Name "SecuritySettings" | Format-List *
```

This command displays all properties of the "SecuritySettings" GPO, such as its unique identifier, creation date, and current status. You can also list all GPOs in your domain with:

```
Get-GPO -All
```

This command is particularly useful when you need an overview of all policies applied across your organization.

Modifying GPO Settings

Once you have a GPO in place, you might need to modify its settings to reflect updated policies. Although many configuration changes are made through the Group Policy Management Editor, you can also modify specific settings using PowerShell. For example, to update a registry-based policy within a GPO, you can use the **Set-GPRegistryValue** cmdlet:

```
Set-GPRegistryValue -Name "SecuritySettings" `
    -Key "HKLM\Software\Policies\Microsoft\Windows\System" `
    -ValueName "DisableCMD" `
    -Type DWORD `
    -Value 1
```

This command configures the "DisableCMD" registry setting in the "SecuritySettings" GPO, effectively disabling the command prompt on target systems.

Linking and Unlinking GPOs

A critical aspect of Group Policy management is linking GPOs to the appropriate Active Directory containers, such as domains, sites, or organizational units (OUs). The **New-GPLink** cmdlet creates a link between a GPO and a target container. For example, to link the "SecuritySettings" GPO to the "OU=Users,DC=yourdomain,DC=com" container, run:

```
New-GPLink -Name "SecuritySettings" -Target
"OU=Users,DC=yourdomain,DC=com"
```

This command ensures that the policy is applied to all users and computers within the specified

OU. If you later decide that the policy is no longer needed, you can unlink it using the **Remove-GPLink** cmdlet:

```
Remove-GPLink -Name "SecuritySettings" -Target
"OU=Users,DC=yourdomain,DC=com"
```

These commands allow you to easily manage where and how policies are applied across your environment.

Removing GPOs

When a GPO is obsolete or no longer required, you can remove it entirely with the **Remove-GPO** cmdlet. For example, to delete the "SecuritySettings" GPO without confirmation, run:

```
Remove-GPO -Name "SecuritySettings" -Confirm:$false
```

Be cautious with this command since removing a GPO is irreversible.

Advanced GPO Management Techniques

For advanced users, the Group Policy module offers additional capabilities. You can combine GPO cmdlets with other PowerShell functions to automate routine tasks. For instance, you might write a script that audits all linked GPOs and exports their settings for review:

```
$gpos = Get-GPO -All

foreach ($gpo in $gpos) {

    $reportPath =
"C:\GPOReports\$($gpo.DisplayName)_Report.html"

    Get-GPOReport -Name $gpo.DisplayName -ReportType HTML -
Path $reportPath

    Write-Host "Report generated for $($gpo.DisplayName):
$reportPath"

}
```

This script iterates through every GPO in your domain, generates an HTML report for each, and saves the report to a specified folder.

Managing Active Directory Sites and Replication

Active Directory Sites are logical groupings of well-connected IP subnets. They help control network traffic and optimize replication by ensuring that domain controllers in the same physical location replicate more frequently than those in different sites. Managing sites effectively ensures that users experience minimal latency and that the directory remains up-to-date across the enterprise.

Creating a New Site

To create a new site, you use the **New-ADSite** cmdlet. For example, to create a site named "NewSite" for a new branch office, run:

```
New-ADSite -Name "NewSite"
```

This command establishes a new site in Active Directory. After creating the site, you may want to configure additional properties such as description or cost, which can help define replication behavior relative to other sites.

Retrieving Site Information

After setting up a site, it is important to verify its properties and ensure it is configured correctly. You can retrieve details using the **Get-ADSite** cmdlet:

```
Get-ADSite -Identity "NewSite"
```

This command outputs information about the site, including its name, cost, and linked subnets.

Modifying Site Attributes

At times, changes in network topology or organizational structure necessitate modifications to site attributes. The **Set-ADSite** cmdlet allows you to update properties such as the site description. For instance:

```
Set-ADSite -Identity "NewSite" -Description "Branch office in NewCity"
```

This command updates the description, providing clarity on the site's purpose and location.

Creating and Managing Subnets

Subnets are integral to the site design, as they define the IP address ranges associated with a particular site. To create a new subnet within a site, you use the **New-ADSubnet** cmdlet. For example, to create a subnet named "NewSubnet" for the "NewSite" with an IPv4 range of "**192.168.0.0/24**," run:

```
New-ADSubnet -Name "NewSubnet" -Site "NewSite" -IPv4Subnet
"192.168.0.0/24"
```

After creation, you can retrieve subnet details with:

```
Get-ADSubnet -Identity "NewSubnet"
```

Modifying a subnet, such as updating its location description, can be achieved with **Set-ADSubnet**:

```
Set-ADSubnet -Identity "NewSubnet" -Location "NewCity Office"
```

These commands ensure that your network topology is accurately represented within Active Directory.

Managing Replication Connections

Replication between domain controllers ensures that changes made in one part of the network are propagated throughout the domain. PowerShell provides several cmdlets to manage these replication connections.

To create a new replication connection between two domain controllers, use **New-ADReplicationConnection**:

```
New-ADReplicationConnection -SourceServer "DC1" -
DestinationServer "DC2"
```

This command sets up a connection that defines how data is replicated from one server to another. To verify the connection, retrieve its details with:

```
Get-ADReplicationConnection -SourceServer "DC1" -
DestinationServer "DC2"
```

If a replication connection needs to be removed—for example, if a server is decommissioned—you can use **Remove-ADReplicationConnection**:

```
Remove-ADReplicationConnection -SourceServer "DC1" -
DestinationServer "DC2" -Confirm:$false
```

These replication management tasks are vital to ensuring that your Active Directory remains synchronized across all sites, reducing the risk of data inconsistencies.

Automating Site and Replication Tasks

To streamline your administrative efforts, consider automating routine tasks related to site and replication management. For instance, you could create a PowerShell script that audits all sites and subnets, generates reports on replication health, and alerts you to any anomalies. An example script might iterate through all sites, check associated subnets, and then validate that replication connections are active:

```
$sites = Get-ADSite -Filter *
foreach ($site in $sites) {
    Write-Host "Site: $($site.Name)"
    $subnets = Get-ADSubnet -Filter * | Where-Object { $_.Site -eq $site.Name }
    foreach ($subnet in $subnets) {
        Write-Host "  Subnet: $($subnet.Name) - IPv4: $($subnet.IPv4Subnet)"
    }
    # Example: Validate replication for domain controllers in this site
    $dcConnections = Get-ADReplicationConnection -Filter * | Where-Object { $_.SourceServer -like "$($site.Name)*" }
    if ($dcConnections) {
        Write-Host "  Replication connections found: $($dcConnections.Count)"
    }
    else {
        Write-Warning "  No replication connections found for site $($site.Name)!"
    }
}
```

This script provides a high-level audit of your site configuration and replication status, allowing you to take corrective action if issues are identified.

Summary

To sum it up, this chapter was all about how to manage Active Directory using PowerShell. You explored the Active Directory PowerShell module, learning its consistent cmdlet naming conventions and powerful capabilities for managing users, groups, computers, and organizational units. You learned how to create, modify, retrieve, and remove AD objects using commands like New-ADUser, Set-ADUser, Get-ADGroup, and Add-ADGroupMember. You practiced how to manage computer accounts, including moving them between organizational units, disabling and removing them, which is key to keeping your network organized.

You also became familiar with managing organizational units, learning how to create, retrieve, modify, rename, move, and delete OUs to reflect the evolving structure of your organization. The chapter also covered managing Group Policy Objects using PowerShell, showing how to create, link, modify, and remove GPOs to enforce policies across your domain. Finally, it showed you how to manage Active Directory sites and replication to ensure that directory information remains consistent and up-to-date across all domain controllers.

CHAPTER 9: POWERSHELL REMOTING

Chapter Overview

This chapter's going to give you the basics of PowerShell Remoting to manage remote systems efficiently and securely. You'll learn how to set up remote sessions using WinRM, including one-to-one and one-to-many connections. This means you can run commands and scripts on multiple machines without needing physical access. You'll see hands-on examples of how to create persistent sessions (PSSessions) that let you run commands over and over again without having to re-establish connections, and how to use implicit remoting to smoothly combine remote cmdlets into your local session.

You'll also dive into secure remote troubleshooting and management, making sure that remote operations are handled with solid error handling and logging. As you go through the chapter, you'll also learn about the best ways to keep your remote sessions safe, like using strong authentication and encrypted communications. By the time you're done with this chapter, you'll have the skills you need to streamline admin tasks, troubleshoot issues across distributed systems, and integrate remote operations into your overall automation strategy.

PowerShell Remoting

PowerShell Remoting is a feature that transforms how you manage remote systems by allowing you to execute commands and run scripts on remote machines directly from your local console. PowerShell Remoting leverages the Windows Remote Management (WinRM) service, which implements the WS-Management protocol to facilitate secure, authenticated communication over HTTP or HTTPS. This functionality is invaluable for system administrators who need to manage multiple machines or perform tasks across different environments without being physically present at each system.

WinRM

At the core of PowerShell Remoting is WinRM, Microsoft's implementation of the WS-Management protocol. WinRM enables you to establish communication between your local machine and remote systems using standard web protocols. This ensures that data exchanged during remote sessions is secure, especially when configured to use HTTPS with proper certificates. In practice, ensuring that WinRM is configured properly on both local and remote machines is the first step to a successful remoting setup.

So here, you might start by verifying that the WinRM service is running and set to start automatically:

```
Set-Service -Name WinRM -StartupType Automatic

Start-Service -Name WinRM
```

Creating and Managing PSSessions

One of the most powerful aspects of PowerShell Remoting is the ability to create persistent sessions, known as PSSessions. A PSSession represents a long-lasting connection to a remote machine, allowing you to execute multiple commands without having to re-establish the connection each time.

You can create a new session using the **New-PSSession** cmdlet:

```
$session = New-PSSession -ComputerName RemoteComputer
```

Here, "RemoteComputer" should be replaced with the remote system's name or IP address. Once a session is established, you can run commands on the remote system by specifying the session:

```
Invoke-Command -Session $session -ScriptBlock { Get-Process }
```

This command retrieves a list of processes from the remote system, demonstrating how PSSessions reduce connection overhead and streamline remote operations.

Implicit Remoting

In addition to explicit session creation, PowerShell offers Implicit Remoting, which allows you to import remote commands into your local session. By using the **Import-PSSession** cmdlet, you can make remote modules available locally as if they were installed on your machine:

```
$importedCommands = Import-PSSession -Session $session -Module
RemoteModule
```

This technique is particularly useful when you need to work with specialized modules on remote systems without having to log into them interactively.

Remote Command Execution and Scriptblocks

Executing commands on remote systems is not limited to interactive sessions. You can run standalone commands or entire scriptblocks using the **Invoke-Command** cmdlet.

```
Invoke-Command -ComputerName RemoteComputer -ScriptBlock {
Get-EventLog -LogName Application -Newest 10 }
```

The command above runs on the remote system and returns the 10 most recent events from the Application log. The use of scriptblocks allows you to bundle multiple commands, include logic, and even define functions that run on remote systems, all from a single command.

Imagine you manage a data center with dozens of servers. Instead of logging into each server individually to perform routine tasks—such as checking disk space, monitoring running processes, or applying updates—you can leverage PowerShell Remoting to execute commands across all servers simultaneously. So lets say, you simply run a script that checks available disk space on each server, which might look like this:

```
$servers = @("Server1", "Server2", "Server3")
Invoke-Command -ComputerName $servers -ScriptBlock {
    Get-PSDrive -PSProvider FileSystem | Select-Object Name,
@{Name="FreeSpace(MB)";Expression={[math]::Round($_.Free/1MB,2
)}}
}
```

This script runs on multiple servers, returning a neat summary of free disk space, thereby saving time and effort compared to manual checks.

The combination of persistent sessions, secure communication, and flexible command execution empowers you to automate complex administrative tasks and troubleshoot systems remotely.

One-to-One Remoting

One-to-One Remoting in PowerShell refers to establishing a connection with a single remote computer to execute commands or run scripts. This focused approach is ideal when you need to troubleshoot a specific machine or perform targeted administrative tasks. We will explore both interactive and non-interactive techniques to connect to a single remote computer, execute commands, and manage the session effectively.

Establishing Interactive Session

Interactive remoting allows you to work on a remote computer as if you were directly logged into it. To begin an interactive session, you use the **Enter-PSSession** cmdlet, which opens a dedicated session with the remote machine.

For example:

```
Enter-PSSession -ComputerName RemoteComputer
```

Once this command is executed, your PowerShell prompt changes to indicate that you are connected to the remote system. You can now run commands, navigate the file system, and perform administrative tasks on the remote machine as if you were physically present.

Now, to exit the interactive session, simply type:

```
Exit-PSSession
```

Non-Interactive Command Execution

Not every task requires a full interactive session. For one-off commands, you can use the **Invoke-Command** cmdlet to execute a scriptblock on a remote computer without entering an interactive session. This method is efficient for running single commands or small scripts.

Consider this example:

```
Invoke-Command -ComputerName RemoteComputer -ScriptBlock {
Get-Process }
```

Here, **Invoke-Command** connects to the remote computer, runs the **Get-Process** cmdlet, and returns the output to your local session. It is less resource-intensive than an interactive session and is ideal for tasks that do not require prolonged interaction.

Handling Remote Sessions with PSSession

Even in one-to-one scenarios, you may benefit from creating a persistent PSSession. By using **New-PSSession**, you establish a session that can be reused for multiple commands:

```
$session = New-PSSession -ComputerName RemoteComputer
```

Once the session is established, you can invoke commands using the **-Session** parameter:

```
Invoke-Command -Session $session -ScriptBlock { Get-Service }
```

This method is efficient for performing a series of related tasks without re-establishing the connection. When you no longer need the session, remove it with:

```
Remove-PSSession -Session $session
```

Sample Program: Remote Troubleshooting

Imagine you need to troubleshoot a server experiencing performance issues. You can use one-to-one remoting to collect data from the server. Begin by establishing an interactive session:

```
Enter-PSSession -ComputerName Server01
```

Inside the session, you might run commands like:

```
Get-Process | Sort-Object -Property CPU -Descending | Select-
Object -First 5

Get-EventLog -LogName System -Newest 20
```

These commands help you identify high-CPU processes and recent system events that could indicate underlying issues. Once you gather the necessary data, exit the session:

```
Exit-PSSession
```

Alternatively, if you prefer a non-interactive approach, you can run the same commands using **Invoke-Command**:

```
Invoke-Command -ComputerName Server01 -ScriptBlock {
    $topProcesses = Get-Process | Sort-Object -Property CPU -
Descending | Select-Object -First 5
    $recentEvents = Get-EventLog -LogName System -Newest 20
    return @{ TopProcesses = $topProcesses; RecentEvents =
$recentEvents }
}
```

This command executes on the remote server and returns the collected data as a structured object, which you can then analyze locally.

So, whether you choose to work interactively or execute commands non-interactively, the techniques you learn here empower you to troubleshoot, configure, and manage individual systems effectively. Security, proper configuration of WinRM, and adherence to best practices ensure that your remote sessions are secure and efficient.

One-to-Many Remoting

Now, One-to-Many Remoting is also a powerful approach to execute commands simultaneously across multiple remote systems. Instead of targeting a single machine, you can specify an array of computers, enabling bulk operations such as software deployment, system health checks, or configuration changes across an entire network segment. This method is particularly useful in large environments where manual intervention on each system is impractical.

Creating List of Remote Machines

One-to-Many Remoting starts by defining the target machines. You can create an array of remote computer names or IP addresses directly in your script. For instance:

```
$RemoteComputers = @("Server01", "Server02", "Server03")
```

Alternatively, if you manage a large number of systems, you can store the list in a text file and import it using:

```
$RemoteComputers = Get-Content -Path
"C:\Path\To\RemoteComputers.txt"
```

Both methods allow you to work with a dynamic list of targets, making your scripts more flexible. Ensure that each remote machine is properly configured for remoting (e.g., WinRM enabled, appropriate firewall rules in place).

Executing Commands across Multiple Machines

With your list of remote machines prepared, you use the **Invoke-Command** cmdlet to execute commands on all specified systems at once. For example, if you want to retrieve a list of running services from each machine, you would run:

```
Invoke-Command -ComputerName $RemoteComputers -ScriptBlock {
Get-Service }
```

In this command, **Invoke-Command** iterates through each computer in **$RemoteComputers**, executing the **Get-Service** cmdlet remotely and collecting the output locally.

Handling Output and Aggregating Results

When running commands on multiple machines, it is essential to handle and aggregate the output effectively. The returned data can be stored in a variable for further processing or reporting. For instance, if you need to analyze disk space on each machine, you might use:

```
$DiskReports = Invoke-Command -ComputerName $RemoteComputers -
ScriptBlock {
    Get-PSDrive -PSProvider FileSystem | Select-Object Name,
@{Name="FreeSpace(MB)";Expression={[math]::Round($_.Free/1MB,2
)}}
}
```

You can then loop through **$DiskReports** to generate a consolidated report, filter out machines with low disk space, or export the data to a CSV file for analysis:

```
$DiskReports | Export-Csv -Path
"C:\Reports\DiskSpaceReport.csv" -NoTypeInformation
```

By aggregating results from multiple machines, you gain a holistic view of your environment and can make informed decisions based on consolidated data.

Advanced Filtering and Error Handling

In one-to-many remoting, not every command may succeed on all remote systems. To handle this gracefully, include error handling and filtering in your script. For example, if some machines might be offline or unresponsive, use the **-ErrorAction** parameter with a try-catch block:

```
$results = Invoke-Command -ComputerName $RemoteComputers -
ScriptBlock {
    try {
        Get-Process -ErrorAction Stop
    }
    catch {
        Write-Output "Error: $_"
    }
} -ErrorAction SilentlyContinue
```

This method ensures that even if errors occur, your script continues executing, and you receive meaningful output for troubleshooting later. Additionally, you can use filtering within the scriptblock to process only specific items, reducing the amount of data you need to handle on your local machine.

Sample Program: Bulk Update Script

Imagine you need to update the time zone setting on multiple servers. Instead of logging into each machine, you can write a one-to-many remoting script. Here's an example:

```
$servers = @("Server01", "Server02", "Server03")
Invoke-Command -ComputerName $servers -ScriptBlock {
    try {
        # Change the time zone to "Pacific Standard Time"
        tzutil /s "Pacific Standard Time"
        Write-Output "Time zone updated successfully on
$env:COMPUTERNAME"
    }
    catch {
```

```
        Write-Output "Failed to update time zone on
$env:COMPUTERNAME: $_"
    }
} -ErrorAction Continue
```

This script connects to each server, applies the time zone change, and outputs the status for each machine. Such bulk operations not only save time but also ensure that updates are consistent across your network.

Sessions and Persistent Connections

While one-to-many remoting is ideal for executing single commands across multiple systems, persistent sessions (PSSessions) allow you to maintain a long-lasting connection to remote computers. These sessions are particularly useful for executing a series of related commands without the overhead of re-establishing a connection for each command. Persistent connections improve performance and enable more complex remote operations, making them essential for advanced administration tasks.

Creating Persistent PSSession

To create a persistent session, use the **New-PSSession** cmdlet. This cmdlet establishes a connection to a remote machine that you can reuse across multiple commands. For example:

```
$session = New-PSSession -ComputerName RemoteComputer
```

This command connects to "RemoteComputer" and stores the session in the **$session** variable. The advantage of using a PSSession is that you can maintain state and context across several commands. This is particularly useful for complex troubleshooting or multi-step administrative processes.

Executing Commands within Persistent Session

Once you have created a persistent session, you can execute commands on the remote computer by specifying the session with the **Invoke-Command** cmdlet:

```
Invoke-Command -Session $session -ScriptBlock { Get-Process }
```

This command runs the **Get-Process** cmdlet on the remote computer using the persistent session, returning the list of processes to your local console. Because the session remains open, you can execute additional commands without re-establishing the connection, thus saving time and reducing overhead.

Entering and Exiting Interactive Sessions

For scenarios where you require direct, real-time interaction with a remote system, you can enter an interactive session using **Enter-PSSession**. This command effectively logs you into the remote computer:

```
Enter-PSSession -Session $session
```

In the interactive session, your prompt changes to reflect the remote system, and you can execute commands as if you were physically present at that machine. When finished, exit the session with:

```
Exit-PSSession
```

Interactive sessions are ideal for ad hoc troubleshooting, while persistent sessions are more suited to scripted, automated tasks.

Importing Remote Commands with Implicit Remoting

Persistent sessions can also be used for implicit remoting. Implicit remoting allows you to import commands from a remote session into your local session, making them appear as local cmdlets.

To do this, use **Import-PSSession**:

```
$importedCommands = Import-PSSession -Session $session -Module
SomeRemoteModule
```

This command imports all cmdlets from "SomeRemoteModule" available on the remote computer into your local session. Implicit remoting is particularly useful when you need to work with modules that are only installed on remote systems.

When you have completed your remote tasks, it is important to properly close and remove persistent sessions to free up resources. You can use **Remove-PSSession** to terminate a session:

```
Remove-PSSession -Session $session
```

Sample Program: Multi-step Remote Administration

Let us think that we need to perform a series of administrative tasks on a remote server—such as checking system health, applying configuration changes, and restarting services. Instead of initiating separate remoting commands for each step, you create a persistent session:

```
$session = New-PSSession -ComputerName "Server01"
```

```
# Check system health
Invoke-Command -Session $session -ScriptBlock {
    Get-Process | Sort-Object -Property CPU -Descending |
Select-Object -First 5
}
# Apply configuration changes
Invoke-Command -Session $session -ScriptBlock {
    Set-ItemProperty -Path "HKLM:\Software\MyApp" -Name
"Config" -Value "UpdatedValue"
}
# Restart a critical service
Invoke-Command -Session $session -ScriptBlock {
    Restart-Service -Name "CriticalService"
}
# Remove the session after completing tasks
Remove-PSSession -Session $session
```

With this, we experience how using a persistent session allows us to chain multiple related tasks efficiently.

Remote Troubleshooting and Management

Remote troubleshooting empowers you to quickly address problems, reduce downtime, and ensure that your environment runs smoothly, regardless of geographic distribution. This topic is very particular to techniques that enable you to diagnose and resolve issues on remote systems without physically accessing each machine. With these techniques, you can gather critical system information, check service statuses, manage processes, and even examine event logs—all from your local workstation.

Gathering System Information

When troubleshooting remotely, obtaining accurate and comprehensive system data is essential. PowerShell Remoting allows you to execute diagnostic commands on remote computers.

For example, to retrieve detailed system information, you might use:

```
Invoke-Command -ComputerName RemoteComputer -ScriptBlock {
Get-ComputerInfo }
```

This command returns data on hardware configuration, OS version, installed updates, and more. Similarly, checking the status of disk space can be done with:

```
Invoke-Command -ComputerName RemoteComputer -ScriptBlock {
Get-PSDrive -PSProvider FileSystem | Select-Object Name,
@{Name="FreeSpace(MB)";Expression={[math]::Round($_.Free/1MB,2
)}} }
```

Such commands provide a snapshot of the remote system's health, which is the first step in effective troubleshooting.

Managing Remote Services

Services often play a critical role in system functionality, and their failure can lead to widespread issues. For example, to check if a critical service like the Windows Update service is running, execute:

```
Invoke-Command -ComputerName RemoteComputer -ScriptBlock {
Get-Service -Name "wuauserv" }
```

If the service is not running, you can start it with:

```
Invoke-Command -ComputerName RemoteComputer -ScriptBlock {
Start-Service -Name "wuauserv" }
```

Monitoring Processes Remotely

If your CPU is using a lot of resources or your apps are unresponsive, it can affect your system's performance. Keeping an eye on processes remotely can help you spot the resource-heavy tasks. You can get a list of running processes sorted by CPU usage with:

```
Invoke-Command -ComputerName RemoteComputer -ScriptBlock {

    Get-Process | Sort-Object -Property CPU -Descending |
Select-Object -First 5

}
```

This command highlights the top processes consuming CPU resources, allowing you to pinpoint potential performance issues. Additionally, if a process is misbehaving, you can remotely terminate it using:

```
Invoke-Command -ComputerName RemoteComputer -ScriptBlock {
Stop-Process -Name "ProcessName" }
```

Inspecting Event Logs for Diagnostics

Event logs provide a wealth of information about system errors, warnings, and informational messages. By remotely accessing these logs, you can diagnose issues without needing to be physically present at the affected machine.

For example, to retrieve the latest 20 error events from the Application log, use:

```
Invoke-Command -ComputerName RemoteComputer -ScriptBlock {
    Get-EventLog -LogName Application -Newest 20 | Where-
Object { $_.EntryType -eq 'Error' }
}
```

This command filters the log entries, allowing you to focus on error events that may reveal underlying issues. You might also export these events for further analysis as shown below:

```
Invoke-Command -ComputerName RemoteComputer -ScriptBlock {
    Get-EventLog -LogName System -Newest 50
} | Export-Csv -Path "C:\Logs\RemoteSystemEvents.csv" -
NoTypeInformation
```

You can export log data for in-depth analysis with other tools or share findings with colleagues for collaborative troubleshooting.

Executing Diagnostic Scripts

In many scenarios, a single command may not suffice to diagnose a complex issue. Instead, you can execute an entire diagnostic script on a remote computer. For example, if you have a script that gathers network configurations, service statuses, and disk usage details, you can run it remotely by specifying the script's file path:

```
Invoke-Command -ComputerName RemoteComputer -FilePath
"C:\Scripts\Diagnostics.ps1"
```

It simplifies troubleshooting by consolidating multiple checks into one script and assures to have consistency across different remote systems.

If you need to do some more in-depth troubleshooting, you can try combining remote command execution with logging and error handling. Try using try-catch blocks in your scriptblocks to capture and report errors that come up during remote operations. Here's an example:

```
Invoke-Command -ComputerName RemoteComputer -ScriptBlock {
    try {
        $processes = Get-Process -ErrorAction Stop
        Write-Output $processes
    }
    catch {
        Write-Error "Failed to retrieve processes: $_"
    }
}
```

Such techniques ensure that your remote troubleshooting is resilient and provides meaningful feedback even when errors occur. Moreover, integrating conditional logic allows you to adjust actions based on the state of the remote system, such as restarting a service only if it has been stopped unexpectedly.

Securing PowerShell Remoting

PowerShell Remoting, while powerful, opens a channel for executing commands on remote machines, which must be protected against unauthorized access and potential security threats.

Secure Communication with WinRM

We know that, the heart of PowerShell Remoting lies in the Windows Remote Management (WinRM) service. Securing WinRM is the first step in protecting your remote sessions. By default, WinRM can be configured to use HTTP, but for enhanced security, you should configure it to use HTTPS. This ensures that all data transmitted between your local machine and the remote system is encrypted.

So, to set up HTTPS for WinRM, you first need an SSL certificate installed on the remote machine. Once you have the certificate, create a new HTTPS listener by running:

```
New-Item -Path WSMan:\LocalHost\Listener -Transport HTTPS -
Address * -CertificateThumbPrint "YourCertificateThumbprint" -
Force
```

Here, you need to replace **"YourCertificateThumbprint"** with the actual thumbprint of your SSL certificate. This command creates a secure listener that encrypts communications, reducing the risk of interception.

Authentication Mechanisms

PowerShell Remoting also supports various authentication methods to ensure that only authorized users can initiate remote sessions. Kerberos is the default and recommended method in domain environments due to its strong security and seamless integration. In non-domain environments, you might use CredSSP or certificate-based authentication.

For instance, to enable CredSSP on the remote machine, run:

```
Enable-WSManCredSSP -Role Server
```

On the local machine, configure the client with:

```
Enable-WSManCredSSP -Role Client -DelegateComputer
"RemoteComputer"
```

Replace **"RemoteComputer"** with the target system's name. These commands enable a more secure delegation of credentials, ensuring that your authentication process remains robust.

Another layer of security involves restricting who can access remote systems. You can limit remote management access by configuring group memberships. For example, add only necessary users to the local "Remote Management Users" group on the remote computer. This minimizes the risk of unauthorized access by ensuring that only trusted administrators can initiate remote sessions. Additionally, implementing Just Enough Administration (JEA) provides granular control over what remote commands users can execute. JEA allows you to delegate only specific tasks to users, without granting them full administrative rights.

Configuring Execution Policies

PowerShell's execution policy is a built-in security feature that restricts the execution of scripts and commands. A strict execution policy, such as **RemoteSigned** or **AllSigned**, helps prevent the execution of untrusted scripts. To configure the execution policy on your local and remote systems, run:

```
Set-ExecutionPolicy RemoteSigned
```

This command enforces that all scripts downloaded from the internet are signed by a trusted publisher, reducing the risk of executing malicious code during remote sessions.

All these best practices ensure that PowerShell Remoting is a powerful tool for remote management, and also a secure and reliable component of your overall system administration strategy.

Summary

To recap, the objectives in this chapter focused on mastering PowerShell Remoting and its various components. You learned how to establish secure connections with remote machines using WinRM and understood the importance of configuring secure communication channels with HTTPS and strong authentication methods. You explored how to create and manage sessions that last, so you can execute commands across one or multiple remote systems, both interactively and non-interactively.

You learned how to use Invoke-Command to run commands, handle one-to-one and one-to-many remoting scenarios, and efficiently troubleshoot and manage remote systems. You also learned some advanced techniques like implicit remoting, which lets you import remote modules into your local session, and best practices for error handling, logging, and security configuration.

CHAPTER 10: POWERSHELL DSC

Chapter Overview

This chapter is going to give you the first introduction to PowerShell DSC. It is a powerful tool for managing and automating system configurations. You'll see how DSC lets you define the desired state of your infrastructure using a declarative syntax, so you don't need to do complex procedural scripting. It'll show you the perks of DSC for system administrators, like better consistency, scalability, and easier troubleshooting. It'll also talk about how DSC helps enforce compliance across both Windows and Linux environments.

You'll learn how to write DSC configurations that generate MOF files and apply them to target nodes using the Local Configuration Manager. It'll also dive into some advanced stuff, like creating custom DSC resources to expand DSC's abilities, so you can handle the unique configurations that your organization needs. At the conclusion of this chapter, you will have a strong understanding of DSC principles and practical techniques to automate complex deployments and maintain a secure infrastructure.

PowerShell DSC Overview

Fundamentals of Desired State Configuration

PowerShell DSC is a declarative management platform that enables administrators to define the desired state of their systems, rather than specifying the step-by-step process to achieve that state. The DSC helps ensure consistency and predictability in configuring servers, workstations, and even cross-platform environments.

At its core, DSC revolves around two major components:

Configuration Scripts

These are specialized PowerShell scripts that define resources and their intended configurations. Instead of detailing how to reach the target setup, you simply describe what the final state should look like. For instance, you might specify that a certain file must exist, a service must be running, or a software package must be installed. DSC resources then translate these declarations into the necessary actions.

Local Configuration Manager (LCM)

The LCM is the engine on each target node (server or workstation) that interprets the configuration scripts. It monitors the system's current state, compares it to the desired state, and makes corrections as needed. If the configuration states that a file should remain present, and someone removes it, the LCM detects the discrepancy and recreates the file. This idempotent model ensures that your systems continuously align with the specified configuration.

DSC uses a simple, readable syntax that lowers the risk of misconfigurations. You can place these scripts under version control, review changes, and roll back if something goes awry. It contrasts with traditional, step-by-step scripting, where administrators must carefully craft each instruction and remain vigilant about dependencies. With DSC, the emphasis shifts to defining outcomes, making the entire configuration process more intuitive and less prone to errors.

Why DSC Matters?

Administrators face numerous challenges: maintaining consistent configurations, managing complex environments, and ensuring security and compliance. DSC alleviates many of these headaches by offering:

- Consistency and Standardization

When you define a DSC configuration, you codify the precise state of your systems. By applying that same configuration script to multiple servers, you enforce a uniform setup. It reduces "configuration drift," where small, untracked changes accumulate over time and lead to unpredictable behaviors. Whether you manage a few servers or hundreds, DSC enforces the same baseline across all nodes.

- Scalability for Large Environments

As environments grow, manual configuration becomes unmanageable. DSC supports automated deployment, allowing you to push a single configuration to many servers simultaneously. You save considerable time compared to logging into each server individually, and you minimize the risk of forgetting steps or making typographical errors on some nodes.

- Version Control and Change Tracking

DSC configurations are ordinary PowerShell scripts, so they can be stored in a version control system such as Git. This setup allows you to track every modification, see who changed what, and revert to earlier configurations if a new setting proves problematic. You gain a complete history of your infrastructure's evolution, which is invaluable for audits and compliance checks.

- Simplified Troubleshooting

Because DSC ensures that machines remain in the declared state, troubleshooting becomes more straightforward. If a node deviates from its configuration, the LCM will attempt to correct the discrepancy. When something truly breaks, you know the system is out of sync with the intended design, making it easier to pinpoint the cause. Administrators spend less time hunting down obscure configuration issues.

- Integration with Existing Tools

DSC is not an all-or-nothing proposition. You can integrate it with popular automation platforms like Chef, Puppet, and Ansible. By layering DSC's declarative capabilities atop your existing workflows, you enhance your automation stack without having to rebuild everything from scratch. This flexibility ensures that DSC can slip seamlessly into many different DevOps pipelines.

- Cross-Platform Capabilities

Although DSC was originally developed for Windows, it now supports Linux as well. If you administer a mixed environment, DSC can unify configuration management under a single approach. This cross-platform support is particularly helpful for teams that want to standardize their automation practices across diverse systems.

- Accelerated Release Cycles

In modern IT, rapid iteration and continuous deployment are often key objectives. By automating configuration tasks, DSC makes it easier to spin up new servers with known-good configurations. This automation reduces friction in the deployment process, letting teams push out changes or new services more rapidly while still maintaining control and consistency.

- Heightened Security

Misconfigurations are a frequent source of security vulnerabilities. DSC mitigates these risks by consistently enforcing security-related settings. You might define firewall rules, user rights, or software patch levels in a configuration, and DSC ensures those rules remain intact. Human error is less likely to introduce a loophole when the system corrects itself automatically.

Evolving with DSC

DSC's design aligns with modern infrastructure-as-code principles. You treat configurations as code—subject to versioning, peer review, and automated testing. This shift fosters collaboration between development and operations teams, supporting a DevOps culture. As your environment evolves, you update DSC configurations, test them in a staging environment, then roll them out to production with confidence.

Administrators who embrace DSC gain not only a powerful tool but also a more strategic perspective on system management. Instead of firefighting individual issues, you define the ideal state once, and DSC maintains it. You free up time to focus on broader initiatives like performance tuning, capacity planning, or new project deployments.

In sum, DSC offers a cohesive, declarative framework for ensuring your Windows or cross-platform environments remain consistent, secure,. and maintainable. It reduces repetitive tasks, lowers the chance of manual errors, and supports agile workflows that drive quicker, safer changes. For any administrator tasked with overseeing a growing infrastructure, DSC can serve as both a time-saver and a reliability booster, transforming how you think about system configuration.

Creating and Deploying DSC Configurations

Designing Configuration Script

When you write a DSC configuration, you define the desired state of a node or set of nodes. You begin by creating a PowerShell script that uses the **Configuration** keyword followed by a name.

Inside the script, you specify:

- Nodes

It indicate which systems you plan to configure. This can be a single machine (like "localhost") or multiple servers defined in an array.

- Resources

Here, you declare each resource you want to manage—files, registry keys, services, or more advanced elements like packages and environment variables.

- Properties

Each resource has properties that determine how it should be configured. For instance, a **File** resource might include **DestinationPath**, **Ensure**, and **Contents** properties to control where the file goes, whether it should exist, and what content it should have.

Following is a simple program:

```
Configuration MySimpleConfig {
    Node 'localhost' {
        File CreateTestFile {
            DestinationPath = 'C:\Test\example.txt'
            Ensure          = 'Present'
            Contents        = 'Hello, DSC!'
        }
    }
}
```

When you run this script as a function (e.g., **MySimpleConfig**), it generates a Managed Object Format (MOF) file. The MOF is the artifact that DSC uses to apply your declared settings.

Generating and Applying MOF File

After defining the configuration, you invoke it like a function:

```
MySimpleConfig
```

PowerShell creates a folder named **.\MySimpleConfig**, containing a **.mof** file (for example, **localhost.mof**) that holds the desired state for the node. To apply the configuration, you use **Start-DscConfiguration**:

```
Start-DscConfiguration -Path .\MySimpleConfig -Wait -Verbose
```

The **-Path** parameter points to the folder where the MOF file is stored, while **-Wait** and **-Verbose** let you watch the process in real time. DSC's LCM reads the MOF file, checks the node's current state, and makes adjustments to match the declared configuration.

Combining Writing and Applying in One Workflow

Many administrators prefer a streamlined workflow where the same script writes the MOF and applies it automatically. You can accomplish this by calling **Start-DscConfiguration** immediately after generating the MOF file.

For example:

```
Configuration MyAutomatedConfig {
    Node 'localhost' {
        Service EnsureW3SVC {
            Name   = 'W3SVC'
            Ensure = 'Running'
        }
    }
}
# Generate the MOF
MyAutomatedConfig
# Apply the MOF
Start-DscConfiguration -Path .\MyAutomatedConfig -Wait -
Verbose
```

It confirms that the entire process—defining, compiling, and applying—happens in one script.

Handling Multiple Nodes and Complex Resources

In real-world scenarios, you might define multiple nodes in a single configuration. For example:

```
Configuration MultiServerConfig {
```

```
    Node 'ServerA', 'ServerB' {
        File SharedFile {
            DestinationPath = 'C:\Data\shared.txt'
            Ensure          = 'Present'
            Contents        = 'Shared config across servers.'
        }
    }
}
```

When you run **MultiServerConfig**, DSC generates two MOF files, one for each server. You can then apply them individually or in a single command if your environment allows it. For advanced tasks, you can incorporate built-in or custom DSC resources. Some resources manage Windows features, while others handle environment variables, registry keys, or package installations.

Verifying and Troubleshooting

After applying a DSC configuration, it's wise to confirm that the node matches the desired state. You might check that a file was created, a service is running, or a registry key is set. If something goes wrong, examine the DSC operational log:

```
Get-WinEvent -LogName "Microsoft-Windows-DSC/Operational" |
Where-Object { $_.LevelDisplayName -eq 'Error' }
```

This log captures errors, warnings, and informational messages related to DSC operations. If you see consistent failures, ensure that your MOF file is valid, the node's LCM is configured properly, and any required DSC resources are present on the node.

Sample Program: Installing Web Server

Let us consider that we want to configure a web server on a Windows machine. For this, we can combine resource declarations in a single DSC script:

```
Configuration WebServerConfig {
    Import-DscResource -ModuleName PSDesiredStateConfiguration
    Node 'MyWebServer' {
        WindowsFeature IIS {
            Name   = 'Web-Server'
```

```
            Ensure = 'Present'
        }
        File WebRoot {
            DestinationPath = 'C:\inetpub\wwwroot\index.html'
            Ensure          = 'Present'
            Contents        = '<html><body><h1>Welcome to
DSC!</h1></body></html>'
        }
    }
}
WebServerConfig
Start-DscConfiguration -Path .\WebServerConfig -Wait -Verbose
```

This script ensures that the Web-Server feature is installed and that the default webpage exists. Once applied, your server is ready to serve the new index page. The declarative nature of DSC frees you from detailing every step, letting you focus on defining the final outcome. As your environment grows, DSC scales with you, providing a stable, automated foundation for your systems.

Creating Custom DSC Resources

The custom DSC resources allow you to define your own configuration logic, enabling you to manage settings that are unique to your environment. It is especially useful when the built-in resources do not cover a particular configuration scenario or when you need to enforce specialized settings across your infrastructure.

Designing Custom Resource

The first step in creating a custom DSC resource is to design it. First, figure out which configuration element you want to manage. For example, say you need to manage the state of a specific Windows service with extra logic that the built-in Service resource doesn't provide. Decide on the properties that the resource will need, like the service name and the desired state (like "Running" or "Stopped"). Clearly defining the specs makes sure you capture everything you need before writing any code.

Implementing Resource

A custom DSC resource typically consists of three key functions: **Get-TargetResource**, **Set-TargetResource**, and **Test-TargetResource**. These functions define how the resource retrieves the current state, applies the desired state, and verifies whether the current state matches the desired configuration.

Below is a sample implementation for a custom DSC resource named **cCustomService**, which manages the state of a Windows service:

```
# cCustomService.psm1
function Get-TargetResource {
    [CmdletBinding()]
    param(
        [Parameter(Mandatory = $true)]
        [string]$Name,
        [ValidateSet("Running", "Stopped")]
        [string]$State
    )

    $service = Get-Service -Name $Name -ErrorAction
SilentlyContinue
    $currentState = if ($service) { $service.Status.ToString()
} else { "NotFound" }

    return @{
        Name  = $Name
        State = $currentState
    }
}
function Set-TargetResource {
    [CmdletBinding()]
    param(
        [Parameter(Mandatory = $true)]
        [string]$Name,
```

```
        [ValidateSet("Running", "Stopped")]
        [string]$State
    )

    $service = Get-Service -Name $Name -ErrorAction
SilentlyContinue
    if ($service) {
        if ($State -eq "Running" -and $service.Status -ne
"Running") {
            Start-Service -Name $Name
        }
        elseif ($State -eq "Stopped" -and $service.Status -ne
"Stopped") {
            Stop-Service -Name $Name
        }
    }
}
function Test-TargetResource {
    [CmdletBinding()]
    [OutputType([System.Boolean])]
    param(
        [Parameter(Mandatory = $true)]
        [string]$Name,
        [ValidateSet("Running", "Stopped")]
        [string]$State
    )

    $service = Get-Service -Name $Name -ErrorAction
SilentlyContinue
    if ($service) {
```

```
        return ($service.Status.ToString() -eq $State)
    }
    else {
        return $false
    }
}
Export-ModuleMember -Function *-TargetResource
```

This script module implements the three required functions. Notice how each function checks the state of the service and performs the appropriate actions. In **Get-TargetResource**, if the service is not found, it returns a "NotFound" state, allowing the DSC engine to handle the discrepancy.

Packaging Resource

Once you've implemented the resource functions, the next step is to package the resource. For this, create a folder named **cCustomService** within a directory like **DSCResources** and place your module file (cCustomService.psm1) and a schema file (cCustomService.schema.mof) in this folder. The schema file defines the structure and properties of your resource.

Following is a simple schema:

```
[ClassVersion("1.0.0"), FriendlyName("cCustomService")]
class cCustomService : OMI_BaseResource
{
    [Key, Description("The name of the Windows service.")]
string Name;
    [Write, Description("The desired state of the service."),
ValueMap{"Running", "Stopped"}, Values{"Running", "Stopped"}]
string State;
};
```

Now here, we need to ensure that our schema accurately reflects the properties required by our resource. Once packaged, we then need to copy the entire **cCustomService** folder to one of the DSC module directories, such as:

- For all users:

```
$env:ProgramFiles\WindowsPowerShell\Modules
```

- For the current user: $env:USERPROFILE\Documents\WindowsPowerShell\Modules

This placement makes the custom resource available to DSC configurations.

Using Custom DSC Resource

After packaging your custom DSC resource, you can use it in a DSC configuration. Create a new DSC configuration script that imports your custom resource and applies it to a target node.

For example:

```
Configuration CustomServiceConfig {
    Import-DscResource -ModuleName "cCustomService" -Name
cCustomService
    Node 'localhost' {
        cCustomService ManageMyService {
            Name  = 'Spooler'
            State = 'Running'
        }
    }
}
CustomServiceConfig
Start-DscConfiguration -Path .\CustomServiceConfig -Wait -
Verbose
```

In this configuration:

- **`Import-DscResource`** brings in your custom resource.
- The **`Node`** block specifies the target machine (in this case, 'localhost').
- The resource instance **`ManageMyService`** ensures that the 'Spooler' service is running.

The DSC engine calls **`Test-TargetResource`** to verify the current state, and if necessary, **`Set-TargetResource`** to bring the service into compliance.

You can extend the power of DSC to cover unique configuration scenarios, automate tailored tasks, and integrate seamlessly with your existing management workflows by creating custom DSC resources. The whole process—design, implementation, packaging, and usage—turns your custom scripts into reusable components that make managing your infrastructure easier.

DSC Configuration Management and Reporting

The DSC Configuration Management and Reporting is a critical aspect of Desired State Configuration that helps you monitor, validate, and report on the state of your infrastructure. DSC not only automates configuration tasks but also provides mechanisms to track compliance and troubleshoot issues. So now, we will learn to manage DSC configurations effectively and generate reports that provide visibility into the configuration status of our nodes.

Managing DSC Configurations

DSC configurations are defined in PowerShell scripts using the **`Configuration`** keyword. Once a configuration is written, you compile it into a MOF file, which the LCM uses to apply settings to target nodes. This process is central to DSC's idempotency—ensuring that configurations are applied consistently, even when re-run multiple times.

To manage configurations:

Write and Compile Configuration

Create a DSC configuration script that specifies the desired state of a node. For example:

```
Configuration WebServerConfig {
    Import-DscResource -ModuleName PSDesiredStateConfiguration
    Node 'localhost' {
        WindowsFeature IIS {
            Name   = 'Web-Server'
            Ensure = 'Present'
        }
        File WebIndex {
            DestinationPath = 'C:\inetpub\wwwroot\index.html'
            Ensure          = 'Present'
            Contents        = '<html><body><h1>Welcome to
DSC!</h1></body></html>'
        }
    }
}
```

Run this configuration to generate the MOF file:

```
WebServerConfig
```

Apply Configuration

Use **Start-DscConfiguration** to apply the MOF to the target node:

```
Start-DscConfiguration -Path .\WebServerConfig -Wait -Verbose
```

The DSC engine compares the current state to the desired state and enforces changes as needed. If the configuration is already applied, DSC makes no modifications, ensuring that changes are idempotent.

Monitoring and Reporting with DSC

Once your DSC configurations are applied, ongoing monitoring is vital to ensure that systems remain compliant with the desired state. DSC provides several tools to help you monitor and report on configuration status.

LCM Logs

The LCM on each node logs its operations, including any errors or deviations from the desired state. You can access these logs using the **Get-WinEvent** cmdlet:

```
Get-WinEvent -LogName 'Microsoft-Windows-DSC/Operational'
```

The filtering these logs by event ID or time range helps you diagnose configuration issues. For example, filtering for error events:

```
Get-WinEvent -LogName 'Microsoft-Windows-DSC/Operational' -
FilterXPath '*[System/EventID=4103]'
```

DSC Reporting with Pull Servers

In large environments, DSC configurations can be distributed via a pull server—a central repository where target nodes periodically check for updated configurations and report their status. Setting up a pull server involves configuring both the server and the target nodes, typically through an LCM configuration script. Once configured, target nodes report their status to the pull server, and administrators can query these reports to assess compliance.

Following is a good example of configuration for a pull server on a target node:

```
[DSCLocalConfigurationManager()]
configuration LCMConfiguration {
```

```
    Node 'localhost' {
        Settings {
            RefreshMode = 'Pull'
            ConfigurationMode = 'ApplyAndAutoCorrect'
            RefreshFrequencyMins = 15
        }
        ConfigurationRepositoryWeb PullServer {
            ServerURL = 'https://your-pull-server-
url:port/PSDSCPullServer.svc'
            RegistrationKey = 'your-registration-key'
        }
        ReportServerWeb PullServer {
            ServerURL = 'https://your-pull-server-
url:port/PSDSCPullServer.svc'
            RegistrationKey = 'your-registration-key'
        }
    }
}
LCMConfiguration
Set-DscLocalConfigurationManager -Path .\LCMConfiguration -
Verbose
```

Here, once your nodes are configured to report to the pull server, you can retrieve status information from the server. This centralized reporting allows you to track compliance across your infrastructure.

Automating Compliance Checks

You can write scripts that regularly query DSC status and generate reports. For example, a script might gather the status of all nodes and export the results to a CSV file for further analysis:

```
$statusReports = Get-DscConfigurationStatus -Detailed
$statusReports | Export-Csv -Path
"C:\DSCReports\ComplianceReport.csv" -NoTypeInformation
```

This command collects detailed configuration statuses and exports them, giving you a snapshot of compliance across your environment.

Sample Program: End-to-End DSC Deployment

Imagine you are responsible for managing a fleet of web servers. You need to ensure that each server has IIS installed, a custom homepage configured, and that all settings remain consistent.

You must:

- Write a DSC configuration that installs the Web-Server feature and configures the homepage.
- Compile the configuration to generate MOF files.
- Apply the configuration to each web server either directly or via a pull server.
- Monitor compliance through LCM logs and periodic status reports.
- Automate the process so that any drift is automatically corrected.

The following script exemplifies this workflow:

```
Configuration WebServerConfig {
    Import-DscResource -ModuleName PSDesiredStateConfiguration
    Node "WebServer01","WebServer02" {
        WindowsFeature IIS {
            Name   = "Web-Server"
            Ensure = "Present"
        }
        File WebIndex {
            DestinationPath = "C:\inetpub\wwwroot\index.html"
            Ensure          = "Present"
            Contents        = "<html><body><h1>Welcome to
DSC!</h1></body></html>"
        }
    }
}
# Generate MOF files
WebServerConfig
# Apply the configuration
```

```
Start-DscConfiguration -Path .\WebServerConfig -Wait -Verbose
# Automate reporting
$status = Get-DscConfigurationStatus -Detailed
$status | Export-Csv -Path
"C:\DSCReports\WebServerCompliance.csv" -NoTypeInformation
```

This script ensures that specified web servers have a consistent configuration and provides a mechanism to report on compliance.

When you add DSC configuration management and reporting to your admin workflows, you get automated, consistent system deployment. These techniques let you not only apply configurations reliably but also monitor compliance and troubleshoot any deviations efficiently. The combination of MOF file generation, pull server reporting, and automated status collection makes sure your infrastructure stays in line with your defined policies, reducing manual effort and enhancing system reliability.

Summary

So, this chapter's all about how PowerShell DSC is this super cool platform for automating and standardizing system configurations. You learned that DSC lets admins define the desired state of their systems using a declarative language, making complex configuration tasks easier. You saw how DSC configurations are written as PowerShell scripts that generate MOF files, which the LCM uses to keep everything consistent across nodes. You explored the benefits of DSC, like standardization, scalability, version control, simple troubleshooting, and better security.

It showed you how to write and apply DSC configurations, including the process of compiling configurations into MOF files and using the Start-DscConfiguration cmdlet to enforce them on target nodes. The chapter also covered creating custom DSC resources, where you designed, implemented, and packaged your own resources to manage configurations unique to your environment. Finally, you learned about DSC configuration management and reporting, including how to monitor, validate, and report on the state of your systems through LCM logs and pull server configurations.

CHAPTER 11: POWERSHELL AND SCCM

Chapter Overview

In this chapter, you'll learn about the integration of PowerShell with System Center Configuration Manager, or SCCM. SCCM is a comprehensive solution for managing Windows-based infrastructure. You'll learn how SCCM centralizes control over devices, applications, and updates while leveraging PowerShell's powerful scripting capabilities to automate and streamline these processes. This chapter will go over the main parts of SCCM, like device collections, deployments, and content distribution, and show you how PowerShell can be used to work with these parts easily. When you put these two together, you can cut down on manual intervention, keep things consistent across your network, and make your IT operations more reliable overall.

In the second part of the chapter, you'll dive into practical steps for using SCCM with PowerShell. You'll learn to load the SCCM PowerShell module, connect to an SCCM site, query and create device collections, deploy applications and software updates, and monitor the status of deployments. You'll check out real-world examples that show how to automate regular tasks and handle big-time deployments using PowerShell scripts. By the time you're done with this chapter, you'll have the skills to use SCCM's full range of features and integrate them with PowerShell to automate more, reduce errors, and improve security and efficiency in your IT environment.

Understanding System Center Configuration Manager

System Center Configuration Manager (SCCM), also known as ConfigMgr or Microsoft Endpoint Manager Configuration Manager (MEMCM), is a comprehensive management solution designed for Windows-based environments. SCCM provides centralized management for deploying, updating, and monitoring operating systems, applications, and devices across an organization. As an IT administrator, you leverage SCCM to ensure that systems remain compliant with organizational policies, receive timely updates, and operate with optimal performance.

Core Components of SCCM

SCCM is built on several key components that work together to manage your IT infrastructure:

- **`Site Server:`** The central component that manages the entire SCCM environment.
- **`Management Point:`** Facilitates communication between client devices and the site server, providing policy and content distribution.
- **`Distribution Points:`** Servers that host and deliver software, updates, and other content to client machines.
- **`Client Agents:`** Installed on managed devices, these agents receive and enforce policies, report status, and perform assigned tasks.

These components form the backbone of SCCM operations to manage everything from operating system deployment to application updates.

SCCM and Automation

SCCM excels at automating complex tasks that would otherwise require significant manual effort. With features such as automated software deployment, patch management, and compliance reporting, SCCM saves administrators valuable time. For instance, SCCM allows you to schedule deployments and updates, ensuring that devices receive the latest software versions without manual intervention. This automation also helps reduce human error, ensuring consistency and reliability across your network.

Integration with PowerShell

One of the standout features of SCCM is its seamless integration with PowerShell. By using the SCCM PowerShell module, you can automate and streamline SCCM operations. This integration empowers you to write scripts that interact directly with SCCM, enabling tasks such as querying device collections, deploying applications, and generating reports. The module includes a variety of cmdlets that adhere to PowerShell's standard Verb-Noun naming convention, making it easier for you to discover and use them. For example, cmdlets like **`Get-CMDeviceCollection`**, **`New-CMDeviceCollection`**, and **`Start-CMApplicationDeployment`** allow you to manage collections and deployments directly from the command line.

SCCM offers numerous benefits for large-scale environments:

- SCCM provides a single console from which you can manage all aspects of your IT infrastructure. This centralization simplifies administrative tasks, improves visibility, and streamlines operations.
- By automating tasks such as software deployment, updates, and inventory management, SCCM reduces manual workload and minimizes the risk of errors. Automated reporting and compliance checks ensure that systems adhere to predefined policies.
- Whether your organization manages a few dozen devices or thousands, SCCM scales to meet your needs. Its architecture supports the distribution of software and updates across vast networks, ensuring efficient operation in large environments.
- SCCM helps maintain a secure environment by enforcing configuration policies, managing software updates, and providing detailed audit trails. These features are essential for compliance with internal and regulatory standards.
- SCCM works well with other Microsoft management tools, such as Windows Server Update Services (WSUS) and Microsoft Endpoint Manager, creating a comprehensive ecosystem for device management and security.

SCCM with PowerShell

Loading SCCM PowerShell Module

Before you can start using PowerShell with SCCM, you need to load the SCCM PowerShell module. The module is typically located within the SCCM installation directories. To load the module, execute the following command:

```
Import-Module (Join-Path $(Split-Path $env:SMS_ADMIN_UI_PATH)
ConfigurationManager.psd1)
```

This command constructs the path to the **ConfigurationManager.psd1** file using the **$env:SMS_ADMIN_UI_PATH** environment variable, which is set by SCCM. Running this command imports all the SCCM-specific cmdlets into your PowerShell session.

To verify that the module is loaded, run:

```
Get-Command -Module ConfigurationManager
```

This command lists all the cmdlets available in the module, ensuring that you have access to the full suite of SCCM commands.

Connecting to SCCM Site

After loading the module, the next step is to connect to an SCCM site. For this, use the **Connect-CMSite** cmdlet as follows:

```
Connect-CMSite -ComputerName SCCMSiteServer -Credential (Get-
Credential)
```

In the above, replace **SCCMSiteServer** with the name of your SCCM site server. When prompted, provide your credentials. This command authenticates you against the SCCM site and sets your session context, enabling you to execute SCCM cmdlets that affect your environment.

Querying Device Collections

Device collections are a fundamental part of SCCM, as they define groups of devices for targeted deployments. To query existing device collections, use the **Get-CMDeviceCollection** cmdlet:

```
Get-CMDeviceCollection
```

This command retrieves all device collections in your SCCM environment, along with details such as collection names, IDs, and member counts. If you need to filter collections, you can use the **-Name** parameter or a filtering expression.

For example:

```
Get-CMDeviceCollection -Name "All Systems"
```

This command returns the device collection named "All Systems," which is typically used as a limiting collection for many deployments.

Creating New Device Collections

If your management tasks require the creation of new device collections, use the **New-CMDeviceCollection** cmdlet. For instance, to create a collection named "New Device Collection" with "All Systems" as the limiting collection, run:

```
New-CMDeviceCollection -Name "New Device Collection" `
    -LimitingCollectionName "All Systems" `
    -RefreshType Periodic `
    -RefreshSchedule (New-CMSchedule -Start "01/01/2023 00:00"
-DayOfWeek Monday -RecurCount 1)
```

This command creates a new device collection that refreshes periodically, based on the schedule defined by **New-CMSchedule**. Adjust the schedule parameters to meet your organizational needs.

Deploying Applications

Th deployment of applications is a common SCCM task that can be automated with PowerShell. To deploy an application, you use the **Start-CMApplicationDeployment** cmdlet. For this, let us consider the following example that deploys an application to a target collection:

```
Start-CMApplicationDeployment -CollectionName "Target
Collection" `
    -Name "Application Name" `
    -DeployAction Install `
    -DeployPurpose Available `
    -UserNotification DisplaySoftwareCenterOnly `
    -AvailableDateTime "01/01/2023 00:00"
```

Just replace the parameters with values appropriate for your deployment scenario. After doing this, this command initiates the deployment process, making the application available to the devices in the specified collection. You can modify parameters like **DeployPurpose** to "Required" if you need a forced installation.

Monitoring Deployments

To monitor deployment, use the **Get-CMDeploymentStatus** cmdlet. First, retrieve the deployment object with **Get-CMDeployment**:

```
$Deployment = Get-CMDeployment -CollectionName "Target
Collection" -ApplicationName "Application Name"
```

Then, check the deployment status:

```
Get-CMDeploymentStatus -DeploymentID $Deployment.DeploymentID
```

This command provides detailed information about the deployment, including success rates, errors, and pending statuses. You can also export this information for further analysis or integrate it into a dashboard for real-time monitoring.

Automating Routine Tasks

One of the main advantages of using PowerShell with SCCM is automation. For routine tasks like updating device collections, deploying recurring applications, or running compliance reports, you can create scripts that execute these tasks on a schedule.

For instance, a script to refresh a device collection might look like:

```
$collection = Get-CMDeviceCollection -Name "New Device
Collection"

if ($collection) {

    Invoke-CimMethod -Namespace "root\SMS\site_<SiteCode>" -
ClassName SMS_Collection -MethodName RefreshCollection -
Arguments @{CollectionID = $collection.CollectionID}

    Write-Host "Device collection refreshed successfully."

}

else {

    Write-Warning "Device collection not found."

}
```

This script retrieves a collection and forces it to refresh using the **Invoke-CimMethod** cmdlet.

Sample Program: End-to-End Deployment Workflow

Let us consider that you are tasked with deploying a new productivity application across your organization. For this, the end-to-end might involve the following steps:

- Import the module and connect to your SCCM site.
- Retrieve the target device collection that will receive the application.
- Initiate the deployment using **`Start-CMApplicationDeployment`**.
- Retrieve and analyze the deployment status to ensure successful rollout.
- Schedule a script to generate periodic reports on deployment compliance.

I have outline a simplified script that encapsulates this workflow. Following is:

```
# Load the SCCM module

Import-Module (Join-Path $(Split-Path $env:SMS_ADMIN_UI_PATH)
ConfigurationManager.psd1)

# Connect to the SCCM site

Connect-CMSite -ComputerName "SCCMSiteServer" -Credential
(Get-Credential)

# Retrieve target device collection

$TargetCollection = Get-CMDeviceCollection -Name "Target
Collection"

# Deploy the application

Start-CMApplicationDeployment -CollectionName
$TargetCollection.Name `

    -Name "Application Name" `

    -DeployAction Install `

    -DeployPurpose Available `

    -UserNotification DisplaySoftwareCenterOnly `

    -AvailableDateTime (Get-Date)

# Monitor deployment status

$Deployment = Get-CMDeployment -CollectionName
$TargetCollection.Name -ApplicationName "Application Name"

$Status = Get-CMDeploymentStatus -DeploymentID
$Deployment.DeploymentID
```

```
$Status | Export-Csv -Path
"C:\DeploymentReports\ApplicationDeploymentStatus.csv" -
NoTypeInformation
Write-Host "Deployment report generated at
C:\DeploymentReports\ApplicationDeploymentStatus.csv"
```

This script shows a smooth, automated process from starting deployment to monitoring and reporting. With scripts like this, you can streamline administrative tasks and ensure that critical software deployments are performed consistently and reliably.

Deploying and Managing Applications

Before you can deploy an application, you must first create it in SCCM. Typically, this is done through the SCCM console, but PowerShell provides automation capabilities to simplify this process. When you create an application, you specify source files, detection methods, and deployment types. For example, you can query the SCCM database to confirm the existence of an application, or even script part of the creation process if the environment supports it. Although most administrators create applications manually using the SCCM wizard, automating subsequent tasks with PowerShell makes managing the deployment more efficient.

Distributing Application Content

Once the application is created, the next step is to distribute its content to Distribution Points (DPs). This ensures that client devices have fast and reliable access to the necessary files. To distribute content, you use the **Start-CMContentDistribution** cmdlet.

A typical workflow involves the following steps:

- Retrieve the application details using **Get-CMApplication**.
- Identify the appropriate Distribution Point using **Get-CMDistributionPoint**.
- Execute the content distribution command.

For example:

```
$Application = Get-CMApplication -Name "My Productivity App"
$DistributionPoint = Get-CMDistributionPoint -
SiteSystemServerName "DPServer01"
Start-CMContentDistribution -ApplicationId $Application.CI_ID
-DistributionPointGroupName $DistributionPoint.GroupName
```

This above script retrieves the application, locates the distribution point, and initiates content distribution. The automation minimizes manual intervention and ensures that content is available on the DPs before deployment begins.

Deploying Application

After distributing content, you deploy the application to a target collection. Device collections in SCCM group devices based on criteria such as location, operating system, or department. Deploying an application involves specifying the target collection, deployment purpose, and scheduling details. You use the **Start-CMApplicationDeployment** cmdlet for this purpose.

Think of the following example:

```
Start-CMApplicationDeployment -CollectionName "Target Devices" `

    -Name "My Productivity App" `

    -DeployAction Install `

    -DeployPurpose Available `

    -UserNotification DisplaySoftwareCenterOnly `

    -AvailableDateTime (Get-Date)
```

In the above command:

- **-CollectionName** specifies the target collection.
- **-Name** refers to the application's display name.
- **-DeployAction** is set to Install.
- **-DeployPurpose** determines whether the deployment is required or available.
- **-UserNotification** controls how users are informed about the deployment.
- **-AvailableDateTime** schedules the deployment start time.

It automates the deployment process such that the application is pushed to all devices in the target collection at the designated time.

Monitoring Application Deployment

Once the deployment is initiated, monitoring its progress is essential to ensure successful rollout. PowerShell provides cmdlets like **Get-CMDeployment** and **Get-CMDeploymentStatus** for tracking deployments. For instance, you can retrieve the deployment object and then query its status:

```
$Deployment = Get-CMDeployment -CollectionName "Target
Devices" -ApplicationName "My Productivity App"
```

```
$Status = Get-CMDeploymentStatus -DeploymentID
$Deployment.DeploymentID

$Status | Format-Table -AutoSize
```

This sequence allows you to review the current status, including successful installations and any errors. Exporting this status to a CSV file for later analysis is also a common practice:

```
$Status | Export-Csv -Path
"C:\DeploymentReports\DeploymentStatus.csv" -NoTypeInformation
```

Automating Deployment Workflows

You can save time and ensure consistency by automating the entire deployment workflow with PowerShell. You can combine the steps above into a single script that

- Loads the SCCM module.
- Connects to the SCCM site.
- Distributes application content.
- Deploys the application to the target collection.
- Monitors the deployment status and generates reports.
- Here's a simplified example of such an integrated workflow:

```
# Load SCCM module

Import-Module (Join-Path $(Split-Path $env:SMS_ADMIN_UI_PATH)
ConfigurationManager.psd1)

# Connect to the SCCM site

Connect-CMSite -ComputerName "SCCMSiteServer" -Credential
(Get-Credential)

# Retrieve application details

$App = Get-CMApplication -Name "My Productivity App"

# Retrieve distribution point details

$DP = Get-CMDistributionPoint -SiteSystemServerName
"DPServer01"

# Distribute application content

Start-CMContentDistribution -ApplicationId $App.CI_ID -
DistributionPointGroupName $DP.GroupName

# Deploy the application
```

```
Start-CMApplicationDeployment -CollectionName "Target Devices"
`
    -Name $App.LocalizedDisplayName `
    -DeployAction Install `
    -DeployPurpose Available `
    -UserNotification DisplaySoftwareCenterOnly `
    -AvailableDateTime (Get-Date)
# Monitor deployment status
$Deployment = Get-CMDeployment -CollectionName "Target
Devices" -ApplicationName $App.LocalizedDisplayName
$Status = Get-CMDeploymentStatus -DeploymentID
$Deployment.DeploymentID
$Status | Export-Csv -Path
"C:\DeploymentReports\DeploymentStatus.csv" -NoTypeInformation
Write-Host "Deployment completed. Report generated at
C:\DeploymentReports\DeploymentStatus.csv"
```

The script above demonstrates how you can use PowerShell to efficiently orchestrate complex deployment tasks. The automation of these operations ensures consistency, reduces manual errors, and enables scalable management of applications.

Managing Software Updates and Patches

Synchronizing Software Updates

The first step in managing software updates is synchronizing the update catalog. This process downloads the latest update information from Microsoft Update or other configured sources. To initiate synchronization using PowerShell, you can use the **Start-CMSoftwareUpdateSync** cmdlet:

```
Start-CMSoftwareUpdateSync
```

This command triggers the synchronization process, ensuring that your SCCM environment is aware of the latest patches and updates.

Creating Software Update Groups

After synchronizing updates, you need to organize them into groups for deployment. A Software Update Group (SUG) allows you to manage updates as a single entity.

To create a new update group, use the **New-CMSoftwareUpdateGroup** cmdlet:

```
$UpdateGroup = New-CMSoftwareUpdateGroup -Name "Critical
Updates Group"
```

This command creates a group where you can later add specific updates.

Adding Updates to Update Group

Once your update group is created, you must populate it with the relevant software updates. You can use the **Get-CMSoftwareUpdate** cmdlet to search for updates that meet certain criteria—such as being classified as "Critical Updates" or "Security Updates"—and then add them to your group using **Add-CMSoftwareUpdateToGroup**. For example:

```
$Updates = Get-CMSoftwareUpdate -DateReleasedMin (Get-
Date).AddMonths(-1) -UpdateClassification "Critical Updates",
"Security Updates"

foreach ($Update in $Updates) {

    Add-CMSoftwareUpdateToGroup -SoftwareUpdateId
$Update.CI_ID -SoftwareUpdateGroupId $UpdateGroup.CI_ID

}
```

This script retrieves updates released in the last month and adds those that are either critical or security-related to the update group.

Deploying Software Updates

With your update group prepared, the next step is to deploy the updates to the target collection of devices. This is achieved using the **Start-CMSoftwareUpdateDeployment** cmdlet. To do this, first, retrieve the target device collection:

```
$TargetCollection = Get-CMDeviceCollection -Name "All
Workstations"
```

Then, deploy the update group to the collection:

```
Start-CMSoftwareUpdateDeployment -SoftwareUpdateGroupName
$UpdateGroup.LocalizedDisplayName `

    -CollectionName $TargetCollection.Name `
```

```
    -DeploymentType Required `
    -SendWakeupPacket $true `
    -UseUtc $true `
    -AvailableDateTime (Get-Date) `
    -DeadlineDateTime (Get-Date).AddDays(7)
```

This command deploys the update group as a required deployment, meaning the updates will be installed automatically. The parameters such as **-AvailableDateTime** and **-DeadlineDateTime** allow you to schedule the deployment, ensuring that updates occur at appropriate times to minimize disruption.

Monitoring Update Deployment

Once the deployment is underway, it is essential to monitor its progress to ensure that updates are installed successfully. For this, use the **Get-CMSoftwareUpdateDeploymentStatus** cmdlet to track the status:

```
$DeploymentStatus = Get-CMSoftwareUpdateDeploymentStatus -
CollectionName $TargetCollection.Name -SoftwareUpdateGroupName
$UpdateGroup.LocalizedDisplayName
```

This command retrieves detailed status information for the deployment, including counts of compliant, non-compliant, and pending updates. You can further process this data to generate reports, for example:

```
$DeploymentStatus | Export-Csv -Path
"C:\UpdateReports\SoftwareUpdateStatus.csv" -NoTypeInformation
```

The exporting of the deployment status to a CSV file allows you to analyze the data and identify any issues that need to be addressed.

In summary, managing software updates and patches with SCCM and PowerShell enables you to maintain a secure, up-to-date environment with minimal manual intervention.

Operating System Deployment Automation

PowerShell combined with SCCM provides a powerful mechanism for automating operating system deployment (OSD). This process automates the installation and configuration of operating systems on devices, allowing you to deploy custom images, configure settings, install applications, and manage drivers consistently across the enterprise. You can also leverage SCCM's task sequences and integrate them with PowerShell scripting to reduce manual intervention and ensure that each deployed system meets your organization's standards.

Creating and Customizing OS Images

The first step in OSD automation is creating a customized OS image that includes your desired configurations, applications, and drivers. This image acts as the baseline for all deployments. Typically, you might use the Microsoft Deployment Toolkit (MDT) or Windows Assessment and Deployment Kit (ADK) to capture an image, but SCCM also provides robust tools for managing these images. Once captured, you can import the image into SCCM and customize it further by adding or removing components. In practice, this image should be tested thoroughly in a lab environment to ensure that all necessary drivers and applications are functioning correctly.

For example, after capturing an image, you would import it into SCCM using the console, and then PowerShell scripts can be used to update image properties or add additional configurations if needed. This preparation ensures that when you deploy the image, the target machines receive an OS that is pre-configured for your environment.

Creating Task Sequence

Task sequences are the heart of OSD in SCCM. They define a series of steps that are executed sequentially to install and configure an operating system on a target device. Each step in the task sequence can perform actions such as partitioning the disk, applying the OS image, installing applications, or running custom scripts.

Although much of the initial setup is typically done through the SCCM console, PowerShell cmdlets like **New-CMTaskSequence** allow you to script part of the process. For example:

```
$TaskSequence = New-CMTaskSequence -Name "Deploy Windows 10" -
Description "Task sequence for deploying Windows 10 with
custom settings"
```

Once the task sequence is created, you can add various steps to it using additional cmdlets. You might add a step to apply the OS image, another to install critical applications, and another to configure post-deployment settings such as joining the domain or applying local policies.

Deploying Task Sequence

After creating and configuring your task sequence, the next step is deploying it to target devices. This involves specifying the device collection that should receive the task sequence using the **New-CMDeviceCollectionDeployment** cmdlet.

For example:

```
$TargetCollection = Get-CMDeviceCollection -Name "All
Workstations"

New-CMDeviceCollectionDeployment -CollectionName
$TargetCollection.Name -TaskSequenceName
$TaskSequence.LocalizedDisplayName -Purpose Required -
SendWakeupPacket $true -DeployAction Install -
AvailableDateTime (Get-Date) -DeadlineDateTime (Get-
Date).AddDays(7)
```

In this example, the task sequence is deployed to the "All Workstations" collection. Parameters like **-AvailableDateTime** and **-DeadlineDateTime** ensure that the deployment occurs within a specific timeframe, providing a controlled rollout. The **-SendWakeupPacket** parameter helps in waking up devices that might be in sleep mode, ensuring they receive the deployment on schedule.

Monitoring Deployment Progress

To be effective, deployment automation requires continuous monitoring to ensure that the task sequence is successfully applied to all target devices. You can use PowerShell to get deployment status using cmdlets such as **Get-CMDeviceTaskSequenceDeploymentStatus**.

For example:

```
$DeploymentStatus = Get-CMDeviceTaskSequenceDeploymentStatus -
CollectionName $TargetCollection.Name -TaskSequenceName
$TaskSequence.LocalizedDisplayName

$DeploymentStatus | Format-Table -AutoSize
```

This command retrieves the status for the deployed task sequence and formats it into a table, making it easier to review key metrics like compliance rates and error counts. You can further automate reporting by exporting these results to a CSV file:

```
$DeploymentStatus | Export-Csv -Path
"C:\OSDReports\DeploymentStatus.csv" -NoTypeInformation
```

Troubleshooting and Error Handling

In any large-scale deployment, errors and issues are inevitable. PowerShell scripts that manage OSD should incorporate robust error handling using try-catch blocks. For example, when applying an OS image, you might include:

```
try {
```

```
    # Apply OS image step
    Invoke-Command -ComputerName $TargetComputer -ScriptBlock
{ Apply-OSImage -ImagePath "C:\Images\Win10.wim" }
    Write-Host "OS image applied successfully on
$TargetComputer."
}
catch {
    Write-Warning "Error applying OS image on $TargetComputer:
$_"
}
```

It ensures that if a particular step fails, the error is logged, and the script continues with the next steps, reducing overall downtime. Additionally, logging each step of the task sequence and reporting errors enables you to diagnose issues faster and refine your deployment process.

SCCM Reporting and Monitoring

To query data, generate reports, and monitor the health and performance of your SCCM environment, PowerShell does help a lot. Both reporting and monitoring are integral to ensuring that deployments, updates, and configuration changes are executed as planned, and to maintaining overall system compliance and performance.

Retrieving Data from SCCM

The first step in generating reports is gathering data from SCCM using the PowerShell module. SCCM provides numerous cmdlets to retrieve information on device collections, deployments, software updates, and more. For example, to retrieve details about all device collections, you can use:

```
$collections = Get-CMDeviceCollection
```

You can filter this data using various parameters. If you need data for a specific collection, such as "All Workstations," run:

```
$targetCollection = Get-CMDeviceCollection -Name "All
Workstations"
```

Similarly, to retrieve software update compliance or application deployment statuses, use cmdlets like **Get-CMSoftwareUpdateDeploymentStatus** and **Get-**

CMDeploymentStatus to compile the necessary information to assess the state of your environment.

Generating Reports

Once you have collected the required data, you can generate reports using PowerShell's built-in formatting and output cmdlets. A common approach is to export the data to CSV or HTML formats for easier consumption and sharing. For example, to generate a report on software update compliance, you might run:

```
$updateStatus = Get-CMSoftwareUpdateDeploymentStatus -
CollectionName $targetCollection.Name -SoftwareUpdateGroupName
"Critical Updates Group"

$updateStatus | Export-Csv -Path
"C:\Reports\UpdateComplianceReport.csv" -NoTypeInformation
```

This command exports the compliance status of software updates for the target collection into a CSV file. You can open this file in Excel or another reporting tool to analyze trends and identify issues.

For a more visually appealing report, you might format the output as HTML:

```
$reportHtml = $updateStatus | ConvertTo-Html -Title "Update
Compliance Report" -PreContent "<h1>Update Compliance for All
Workstations</h1>"

$reportHtml | Out-File -FilePath
"C:\Reports\UpdateComplianceReport.html"
```

This command converts the data into an HTML document with a custom title and header, making it easier to share with stakeholders.

Automating Reporting Tasks

To ensure that reports are generated regularly, you can schedule PowerShell scripts to run at predefined intervals using Task Scheduler. It can monitor SCCM deployments, update compliance, and other key metrics on an ongoing basis without manual intervention.

For example, a script might collect deployment statuses and export a daily report:

```
# Retrieve collection and deployment data

$collections = Get-CMDeviceCollection

$deploymentData = foreach ($col in $collections) {
```

```
    Get-CMDeployment -CollectionName $col.Name
}
# Export the consolidated report to CSV
$deploymentData | Export-Csv -Path
"C:\Reports\DailyDeploymentReport.csv" -NoTypeInformation
```

This script can run every day at midnight in order to have a fresh report each morning for review.

Monitoring Deployment and Update Health

Beyond generating static reports, ongoing monitoring is critical for proactive management. You can use PowerShell scripts to query real-time data from SCCM, such as the status of current deployments, software update compliance, and even hardware inventory. For example, a real-time monitoring script might display deployment statuses in the console:

```
$deployments = Get-CMDeployment -CollectionName "All
Workstations"
$deployments | Format-Table -Property Name, DeploymentID,
Status, LastModifiedTime -AutoSize
```

This command provides a snapshot of all deployments, allowing you to quickly identify any that are failing or pending action.

For environments that require real-time monitoring and alerting, you may integrate PowerShell with monitoring frameworks or email notifications. You can use cmdlets like **Send-MailMessage** to send alerts when specific thresholds are met, such as a deployment failure rate exceeding a certain percentage.

Summary

In summary, the lessons in this chapter focused on integrating PowerShell with SCCM to streamline IT management tasks. You learned about SCCM's role as a comprehensive solution for managing devices, applications, and updates in Windows environments and how its various components work together to provide centralized control. You discovered how to load the SCCM PowerShell module, connect to an SCCM site, and perform key tasks such as querying and creating device collections, deploying applications, and monitoring deployments. You also explored techniques for managing software updates and patches, automating operating system deployment, and generating detailed reports through PowerShell. These methods allowed you to automate routine tasks, reduce manual errors, and maintain a consistent, secure IT environment.

CHAPTER 12: POWERSHELL SECURITY AND BEST PRACTICES

Chapter Overview

This chapter will show you the key security practices you need to protect your PowerShell environment and scripts. It shows you how to implement secure coding practices-such as validating input, avoiding hard-coded credentials, and applying the principle of least privilege-to minimize vulnerabilities and prevent exploitation. You'll take a look at PowerShell's execution policy settings, which control how and when scripts are allowed to run, ensuring that only trusted code is executed.

You'll then dive into more advanced security measures designed to restrict potential attack vectors. We'll cover features like Constrained Language Mode, which limits PowerShell's capabilities to a safe subset, and Just Enough Administration (JEA), which enforces role-based access control to restrict user actions. You'll learn how to set up auditing and logging to track PowerShell activities, so you can proactively monitor and respond to incidents quickly. By the time you're done with this chapter, you should have all the skills to implement solid security controls and best practices. That way, you can make sure that your automation efforts stay safe and compliant in today's complicated IT environments.

Secure Coding Practices

As you develop and deploy scripts that can control critical system components, it becomes imperative to ensure that your code does not inadvertently introduce vulnerabilities. WE will now explore some of the techniques and best practices that help you safeguard your scripts, mitigate risks from potential cyber-attacks, and provide the integrity of your automation processes.

Minimizing Hardcoded Credentials

One of the most common pitfalls in scripting is the use of hardcoded credentials. Hardcoding sensitive data, such as usernames and passwords, directly into your scripts exposes them to unauthorized access. To mitigate this risk, you should avoid embedding credentials in plain text. Instead, use secure storage solutions like the Windows Credential Manager or Azure Key Vault.

Simply make use of the **Get-Credential** cmdlet to prompt for credentials at runtime as below.

```
$Creds = Get-Credential
```

You can also store credentials in encrypted files using the **Export-Clixml** and **Import-Clixml** cmdlets. It encrypts the data based on the current user context, reducing exposure risks.

```
# Saving credentials securely
$Creds | Export-Clixml -Path "C:\Secure\creds.xml"
```

```
# Loading credentials securely
$Creds = Import-Clixml -Path "C:\Secure\creds.xml"
```

Validating Input Data

PowerShell scripts frequently rely on external inputs such as user entries, configuration files, or command-line parameters. Unvalidated input can lead to injection attacks or other security breaches. Utilize PowerShell's built-in validation attributes to enforce constraints on your inputs.

ValidatePattern

This attribute ensures that strings match a specific regular expression. For instance, to validate a file path:

```
param(
    [Parameter(Mandatory=$true)]
    [ValidatePattern("^([A-Za-z]:\\).+")]
    [string]$FilePath
)
```

ValidateSet

Restrict input to a predefined set of values:

```
param(
    [Parameter(Mandatory=$true)]
    [ValidateSet("Running", "Stopped")]
    [string]$ServiceState
)
```

These validations prevent unexpected or malicious data from being processed.

Using Signed Scripts and Execution Policies

Script signing is a robust method to verify that a script has not been tampered with. Digital signatures authenticate the source of the script and guarantee its integrity. When you sign your scripts with a trusted certificate, you reduce the risk of malicious modifications.

Signing Script

To do this, use the **Set-AuthenticodeSignature** cmdlet to sign your script:

```
Set-AuthenticodeSignature -FilePath "C:\Scripts\MyScript.ps1"
-Certificate (Get-Item Cert:\CurrentUser\My\<Thumbprint>)
```

Execution Policies

You need to rely on PowerShell's execution policies (discussed in detail in the next section) to ensure that only signed and trusted scripts are executed. After this, setting policies to "AllSigned" or "RemoteSigned" adds an extra layer of security.

PowerShell Execution Policy

PowerShell Execution Policy is a built-in security feature that controls the conditions under which PowerShell loads configuration files and executes scripts. This feature is designed to protect your system from executing malicious or unauthorized scripts.

Predefined Execution Policies

PowerShell offers several predefined execution policies, each with a different level of security. The most commonly used policies include:

- Restricted

The default policy for Windows client computers, which does not allow any scripts to run. Only individual commands can be executed interactively.

- AllSigned

It permits the execution of scripts only if they are signed by a trusted publisher. This ensures that every script has been reviewed and verified for authenticity before execution.

- RemoteSigned

This allows locally created scripts to run without a signature. However, scripts downloaded from the internet or received via email must be signed by a trusted publisher. This policy strikes a balance between security and convenience.

- Unrestricted

This permits all scripts to run regardless of their origin or signature status. This policy offers the least security and is generally not recommended for production environments.

- Bypass

This disables all script execution restrictions, meaning that PowerShell will run any script without warning. This is rarely used except for temporary, controlled scenarios.

- Undefined

It indicates that no execution policy has been set. When the policy is undefined, the system defaults to Restricted (on clients) or a configured default on servers.

These policies determine the level of risk your system is exposed to. For most production environments, **RemoteSigned** or **AllSigned** is recommended to provide a balance between security and usability.

Configuring Execution Policy

Now here, the change of execution policy is done using the **Set-ExecutionPolicy** cmdlet. This command must be run in an elevated PowerShell session (Run as Administrator). For example, to set the execution policy to RemoteSigned, use:

```
Set-ExecutionPolicy RemoteSigned
```

After running this command, PowerShell prompts you to confirm the change. Confirming the change updates the policy, which you can verify by running:

```
Get-ExecutionPolicy
```

This command returns the current execution policy, confirming that your settings have been applied.

Bypassing Execution Policy Temporarily

In certain scenarios, you might need to run a script that is blocked by the current execution policy. Instead of permanently lowering the security settings, you can bypass the execution policy for a single session. This is achieved by launching PowerShell with the **-ExecutionPolicy Bypass** parameter.

For example:

```
PowerShell.exe -ExecutionPolicy Bypass -File
"C:\Path\To\Script.ps1"
```

This command runs the specified script with the execution policy bypassed, without changing the system-wide settings. This temporary bypass is useful for running trusted scripts that are blocked by stricter policies.

Sample Program: Changing and Verifying Execution Policy

Let us think of a situation where you need to deploy a new script across your organization, but your current execution policy is too restrictive. Now here, you can create a script to check the current policy, change it if necessary, and then verify the update.

Following is a sample script named **ChangeExecutionPolicy.ps1**:

```
# Define the desired policy
$DesiredPolicy = "RemoteSigned"
# Retrieve the current execution policy
$currentPolicy = Get-ExecutionPolicy
if ($currentPolicy -ne $DesiredPolicy) {
    Write-Output "Current policy is $currentPolicy. Changing
to $DesiredPolicy..."
    Set-ExecutionPolicy $DesiredPolicy -Force
    Write-Output "Execution policy changed to $(Get-
ExecutionPolicy)."
} else {
    Write-Output "Execution policy is already set to
$DesiredPolicy."
}
```

Now when you run this script in an elevated PowerShell session, it checks the current execution policy, updates it if necessary, and confirms the change. It ensures that you maintain the required security posture while still allowing your scripts to run.

Constrained Language Mode

Constrained Language Mode (CLM) is a security feature in PowerShell designed to restrict the capabilities of the scripting language, thereby reducing the potential for abuse by attackers. In environments where security is paramount, CLM limits the available language features to a safe subset. This helps prevent attackers from leveraging advanced PowerShell features—such as direct .NET method invocations, dynamic type creation, or certain API calls—to execute malicious actions.

How CLM Works?

When CLM is enabled, PowerShell restricts several elements of the language:

- The access to .NET types and methods is curtailed. Only a predefined, safe subset of .NET functionality is available, which minimizes the risk of invoking dangerous methods.

- Some of the advanced language features, including the use of **`Add-Type`**, **`New-Object`**, and **`Invoke-Expression`**, are disabled. This means that even if a script contains potentially harmful code, these commands cannot execute.
- The script block logging and invocation restrictions are imposed, ensuring that potentially dangerous operations are either logged or entirely blocked.

All these limitations are typically enforced via Windows Defender Application Control (WDAC), AppLocker, or Device Guard policies. In highly secure environments, administrators use CLM to ensure that only approved, limited functionality is available to less-trusted users or scripts.

Enabling and Disabling CLM

Enabling CLM is usually done through group policies or by configuring WDAC/AppLocker settings on your system. For instance, within an enterprise environment, you might enforce CLM by setting an AppLocker policy that restricts PowerShell to a constrained mode. Here's a high-level overview of the steps:

- **Group Policy Configuration:**

- Open the Group Policy Management Editor (gpedit.msc) and navigate to "Computer Configuration" > "Policies" > "Windows Settings" > "Security Settings" > "Application Control Policies" > "AppLocker". Under the PowerShell section, set the policy to enforce CLM.

- **Device Guard/WDAC:**

- Configure Device Guard or WDAC to limit the execution of PowerShell to a constrained set of functionalities. This involves creating and deploying a policy that defines the allowed commands and language features.

On the other hand, disabling CLM should only be done when it's really necessary and you're aware of the risks. It's usually for trusted admins who need the full language features for advanced troubleshooting or script development.

Implementing Just Enough Administration

Just Enough Administration-or JEA-is a security framework within PowerShell that lets organizations delegate admin tasks without giving users full admin privileges. When you use JEA, you can limit what users can do, making sure they can get the job done without messing up the system. JEA is based on the idea of least privilege, meaning users only have the access they need to get the job done.

How JEA Works?

JEA works by creating a restricted PowerShell session configuration that defines which commands, functions, and external scripts a user can execute. This configuration is encapsulated in two primary components:

- **Role Capability Files (.psrc):** These files specify the commands and functions that are visible to users assigned to a particular role. They define what the user can do when they connect to a JEA endpoint.
- **Session Configuration Files (.pssc):** These files establish the session environment, including settings such as the virtual account under which commands run, logging preferences, and mappings to role capability files. The session configuration controls the overall behavior of the JEA endpoint.

Together, these components create a sandboxed environment where users can perform only the actions defined in the role capability file. For example, you might create a JEA configuration for helpdesk administrators that allows them to query Active Directory user objects and reset passwords, but not to change group memberships or alter critical system configurations.

Creating Role Capability File

Now to implement JEA, we need to start by defining a role capability file. This file specifies which cmdlets, functions, and scripts are allowed for a specific role. You can use the **New-PSRoleCapabilityFile** cmdlet to generate a new role capability file as below:

```
New-PSRoleCapabilityFile -Path
"C:\JEA\RoleCapabilities\HelpDesk.psrc"
```

After generating the file, edit it to define the allowed commands. Following is a simple example for a HelpDesk role:

```
@{
    GUID = '12345678-1234-1234-1234-123456789abc'
    ModulesToImport = @('ActiveDirectory')
    VisibleCmdlets = @('Get-ADUser', 'Set-ADAccountPassword',
'Unlock-ADAccount')
    VisibleFunctions = @()
    VisibleExternalCommands =
@('C:\Windows\System32\ping.exe')
}
```

In this file, you specify that members of the HelpDesk role can import the ActiveDirectory module and use specific cmdlets such as **Get-ADUser**, **Set-ADAccountPassword**, and **Unlock-ADAccount**. The GUID is a unique identifier for the role capability.

Creating Session Configuration File

Next, you need to create a session configuration file that defines the JEA endpoint. This file associates the role capability with specific users or groups and configures the session environment. You can use the **New-PSSessionConfigurationFile** cmdlet to create a new file:

```
New-PSSessionConfigurationFile -Path
"C:\JEA\SessionConfigurations\HelpDesk.pssc" `
    -SessionType RestrictedRemoteServer `
    -RunAsVirtualAccount `
    -RoleDefinitions @{ 'CONTOSO\HelpDesk' = @{
'RoleCapabilities' = 'HelpDesk' } }
```

Here,

- The configuration file sets up a JEA endpoint named "HelpDesk" that restricts users in the **CONTOSO\HelpDesk** group to only the commands specified in the HelpDesk role capability file.
- The **-RunAsVirtualAccount** parameter ensures that the commands execute under a temporary, isolated account, further enhancing security.

Registering and Testing JEA Endpoint

Once your role capability and session configuration files are ready, you need to register the JEA endpoint. You can use the **Register-PSSessionConfiguration** cmdlet to do this:

```
Register-PSSessionConfiguration -Name "HelpDesk" -Path
"C:\JEA\SessionConfigurations\HelpDesk.pssc" -Force
```

This command registers the endpoint, making it available for remote connections. Administrators and helpdesk personnel can now connect to the JEA endpoint using the specified configuration.

Now to verify that your JEA endpoint works as intended, we need to initiate a remote session using **Enter-PSSession**:

```
Enter-PSSession -ComputerName "ServerName" -ConfigurationName
"HelpDesk" -Credential (Get-Credential)
```

Here, you simply replace "ServerName" with the target server's name. When connected, the user will be restricted to the commands defined in the role capability file. This limited access ensures that even if an account is compromised, the potential damage is minimized. Once testing is complete, exit the session with:

```
Exit-PSSession
```

When you use JEA, you set up a protected, limited environment for remote administration that follows the principle of least privilege. This not only makes things more secure, but it also gives you a controlled way to delegate specific tasks without having to use all of PowerShell's features.

DSC Configuration Management and Reporting

We now move on to explore how to manage DSC configurations and generate reports. It is a critical aspect of maintaining infrastructure compliance and ensuring that systems remain in their desired state. DSC configuration management involves applying configuration scripts, monitoring system compliance, and generating reports that provide insights into the state of your environment.

Managing DSC Configurations

DSC configurations are defined in PowerShell scripts and compiled into MOF files that the LCM uses to enforce settings on target nodes. You write a configuration using the **Configuration** keyword, specifying the target nodes and desired resources. For example, a simple configuration might ensure that a particular file exists or that a service is running. Once the configuration script is executed, PowerShell generates the corresponding MOF file, which is then applied to the node using **Start-DscConfiguration**.

```
Configuration WebServerConfig {
    Import-DscResource -ModuleName PSDesiredStateConfiguration
    Node "localhost" {
        WindowsFeature IIS {
            Name   = "Web-Server"
            Ensure = "Present"
        }
        File WebIndex {
            DestinationPath = "C:\inetpub\wwwroot\index.html"
            Ensure          = "Present"
            Contents        = "<html><body><h1>Welcome to
DSC!</h1></body></html>"
        }
```

```
    }
}
WebServerConfig
Start-DscConfiguration -Path .\WebServerConfig -Wait -Verbose
```

This configuration ensures that the IIS feature is installed and that a default webpage is present. DSC's idempotent design guarantees that the configuration will be reapplied only when deviations are detected.

Generating and Managing Reports

Once your DSC configurations are deployed, continuous monitoring is essential. The LCM on each node logs its actions, and you can retrieve these logs to assess compliance. The **Get-WinEvent** cmdlet can be used to extract DSC-related events from the "Microsoft-Windows-DSC/Operational" log.

```
Get-WinEvent -LogName 'Microsoft-Windows-DSC/Operational'
```

By filtering these logs with specific event IDs or conditions, you can pinpoint errors or confirm successful resource applications. For instance:

```
Get-WinEvent -LogName 'Microsoft-Windows-DSC/Operational' -
FilterXPath '*[System/EventID=4103]'
```

This command retrieves events indicating successful resource configurations, which are vital for verifying that your systems are in the desired state.

Using Pull Servers

In large environments, DSC configurations are often deployed via a pull server. A pull server not only distributes MOF files to target nodes but also collects status reports from these nodes. This centralized approach enables you to monitor compliance across your entire infrastructure. Configuring a pull server involves setting up a repository where nodes periodically check for updates and send back their status reports.

A basic configuration for a pull server might be defined as follows:

```
[DSCLocalConfigurationManager()]
configuration LCMConfiguration {
    Node 'localhost' {
        Settings {
```

```
            RefreshMode = 'Pull'
            ConfigurationMode = 'ApplyAndAutoCorrect'
            RefreshFrequencyMins = 15
        }
        ConfigurationRepositoryWeb PullServer {
            ServerURL = 'https://your-pull-server-
url:port/PSDSCPullServer.svc'
            RegistrationKey = 'your-registration-key'
        }
        ReportServerWeb PullServer {
            ServerURL = 'https://your-pull-server-
url:port/PSDSCPullServer.svc'
            RegistrationKey = 'your-registration-key'
        }
    }
}
LCMConfiguration
Set-DscLocalConfigurationManager -Path .\LCMConfiguration -
Verbose
```

Once your nodes are configured to report to the pull server, you can aggregate compliance data centrally and generate comprehensive reports on system health.

Automating Reporting Tasks

The PowerShell scripts can be scheduled to run at regular intervals, gathering DSC compliance data and generating reports. For example, a script might collect status information from all nodes, format the data, and export it to a CSV file for analysis:

```
$StatusReports = Get-DscConfigurationStatus -Detailed
$StatusReports | Export-Csv -Path
"C:\DSCReports\ComplianceReport.csv" -NoTypeInformation
```

The automated reporting ensures that you have up-to-date information at your fingertips, making it easier to identify problems early and take corrective action.

For a more interactive and detailed view, you can convert compliance data into HTML reports or dashboards. For instance, converting a CSV report to an HTML format provides a visually appealing summary that can be shared with stakeholders:

```
$reportHtml = $StatusReports | ConvertTo-Html -Title "DSC
Compliance Report" -PreContent "<h1>DSC Compliance
Overview</h1>"

$reportHtml | Out-File -FilePath
"C:\DSCReports\ComplianceReport.html"
```

These reports can include tables, charts, or even embedded links to detailed logs, offering a holistic view of your configuration management status.

Summary

This chapter focused on how to improve PowerShell security and the best ways to do it. You learned to implement secure coding practices by avoiding hardcoded credentials, validating inputs rigorously, and employing the principle of least privilege. You also discovered how to use digital signatures and execution policies to control which scripts are allowed to run, thereby protecting your systems from malicious code. You explored advanced error handling and logging techniques to make sure that any issues are found and documented quickly for auditing and troubleshooting. You also explored advanced security measures like Constrained Language Mode, which limits PowerShell functionality to a safe subset, and Just Enough Administration (JEA), which limits user privileges to only what's necessary for specific tasks. All of these measures worked together to boost your security and help you keep PowerShell in a stronger, more controlled state.

CHAPTER 13: ADVANCED POWERSHELL TECHNIQUES

Chapter Overview

This chapter's got some advanced PowerShell techniques that'll totally transform your scripting abilities and take your automation strategies to the next level. It explores the power of regular expressions for complex text manipulation, allowing you to search, replace, and extract data with precision. You delve into handling structured data formats such as XML and JSON, allowing for seamless integration with web services and configuration files. You'll also learn to use multithreading and parallel processing, which will let you do tasks at the same time and make your performance way better. As you go along, you'll create custom cmdlets and modules that capture complex logic into reusable components, and you'll bring the full power of the .NET framework into your scripts, expanding PowerShell's capabilities beyond its built-in functions.

You'll also see how these advanced techniques are used to solve real-world problems, like processing large data sets and building automation workflows that can be scaled up. By the time you're done with this chapter, you'll be able to handle complex tasks in different environments, making your PowerShell-based automation projects more reliable, scalable, and easy to maintain.

Advanced PowerShell Techniques

PowerShell started as a simple scripting language, but it's now a solid automation and configuration platform that a lot of modern IT environments use. While basic scripting skills can handle day-to-day admin tasks, some scenarios need more advanced techniques for complex data manipulation, parallel execution, or custom command development.

Why Advanced Techniques?

Advanced PowerShell techniques are the key to linking basic scripting with enterprise-grade automation solutions. As your environment grows in size and complexity, so do your automation requirements. You can use techniques like sophisticated text manipulation, parallel processing, creating custom modules, and interacting with external data formats to manage large-scale operations more efficiently. Whether you're handling multi-server deployments, working with massive log files, or building custom tools for your organization, these advanced features help you keep things running smoothly, cut down on errors, and streamline your processes.

There's a bunch of different areas where the PowerShell ecosystem shines, like:

- Text Manipulation and Regular Expressions

Regular expressions empower you to search, validate, and transform text with incredible precision. Coupled with PowerShell's native string operations, you can handle complex data extraction or reformatting tasks that might otherwise require specialized scripting languages.

- Handling Structured Data

XML and JSON are staples of modern data interchange. PowerShell's built-in cmdlets simplify parsing and creating these formats, letting you work seamlessly with APIs, configuration files, and other structured data sources.

- Concurrency and Parallelism

Techniques like the **`ForEach-Object -Parallel`** parameter, background jobs, or even .NET concurrency classes enable you to process tasks concurrently. This improves performance in scenarios where scripts handle large data sets or perform I/O-bound tasks.

- Custom Cmdlets and Modules

For specialized tasks, building your own cmdlets in PowerShell or .NET can encapsulate functionality into reusable commands. Modules then bundle related cmdlets and scripts for easy sharing and versioning.

- Integration with .NET

PowerShell's deep integration with the .NET framework means you can tap into a vast ecosystem of classes and libraries. This extends PowerShell's capabilities to advanced GUI interactions, custom data structures, or specialized APIs.

When to Use Advanced Techniques

You do not always need advanced techniques for everyday tasks. However, as soon as you encounter:

- Large Data Processing

For parsing massive log files or handling big data sets, advanced text manipulation and concurrency can drastically reduce processing time.

- Complex Application Integrations

When bridging multiple systems or APIs, you may need to parse or generate XML/JSON, build custom modules, or rely on .NET libraries to interact with external services.

- Enterprise-Scale Automation

Deploying software or configurations across thousands of devices, or orchestrating tasks that require robust error handling and concurrency, often calls for advanced features.

- Custom Tooling

If your scripts evolve into internal tools that multiple teams rely on, converting them into custom cmdlets or modules helps maintain consistency, manage updates, and integrate them seamlessly into the PowerShell ecosystem.

With this high-level overview in mind, let's dive into the first advanced topic: using regular expressions for sophisticated text manipulation.

Regular Expressions and Text Manipulation

Regular expressions (regex) are a powerful language for pattern matching and text processing. PowerShell integrates regex capabilities through operators like **-match** and **-replace**, cmdlets such as **Select-String**, and the .NET **[regex]** class. Whether you need to parse log files, validate input, or transform strings, regex offers unmatched flexibility for matching and rewriting text.

Basic Regex Concepts

A Regex pattern is made up of literal characters and special symbols (meta characters) that define the shape of the text you are searching for. Some basic elements include:

- **Literal Characters**: Letters, digits, or symbols that match themselves (e.g., **abc**).
- **Character Classes**: Defined with brackets, **[ ]**, to match any one character within a specified set (e.g., **[aeiou]**).
- **Quantifiers**: Indicate how many times a pattern should repeat. For example, **+** (one or more), ***** (zero or more), **?** (zero or one), and **{n}** (exact count).
- **Anchors**: **^** matches the start of a line, and **$** matches the end of a line. **\b** denotes a word boundary, which is helpful for matching whole words.

All these elements helps to build patterns that identify exactly the strings you need.

Using '-match' Operator

The **-match** operator in PowerShell checks if a string contains a match for a given regex pattern. If the pattern is found, **$true** is returned, and the **$matches** automatic variable is populated with details about the match.

For example:

```
$text = "PowerShell is fun!"
$pattern = "\b\w{5}\b"
if ($text -match $pattern) {
    Write-Host "Match found: $($matches[0])"
} else {
    Write-Host "No match found"
}
```

Here, the pattern **\b\w{5}\b** looks for a five-letter word. If found, **$matches[0]** returns the matched substring, such as "Power" in "PowerShell."

'-replace' Operator

For rewriting strings based on regex matches, use the **-replace** operator. It replaces all occurrences of a pattern with a specified replacement:

```
$text = "My phone number is 123-456-7890."
$newText = $text -replace "\d", "*"
Write-Host $newText
```

Here, every digit (**\d**) in the text is replaced with an asterisk. The result might be **My phone number is ***-***-****.**

'Select-String' Cmdlet

PowerShell's **Select-String** cmdlet acts like the grep utility, searching for a regex pattern in files or strings. For example, to search for lines containing "Error" in all **.log** files:

```
Select-String -Path "C:\Logs\*.log" -Pattern "Error"
```

The **Select-String** outputs matching lines along with file and line number information. It can also be piped to other cmdlets for further processing.

Advanced Regex

When you need more granular control or advanced features, the **[regex]** .NET class is available. This class offers methods like **Matches()**, **Split()**, and **Replace()**. For instance, **Matches()** returns all match objects, which you can iterate over to extract subgroups or handle partial matches:

```
$text = "IDs: 123, 456, and 789"
$pattern = "\d+"
$allMatches = [regex]::Matches($text, $pattern)
foreach ($m in $allMatches) {
    Write-Host "Found number: $($m.Value)"
}
```

Similarly, **[regex]::Split()** and **[regex]::Replace()** allow you to define more sophisticated logic than the **-replace** operator, including custom delegates or script blocks to handle each match differently.

Sample Program: Parsing Log Entries

Following is an example of how you might go about parsing a system log file to get the date, time, and error codes:

```
$logEntries = Get-Content "C:\Logs\SystemLog.txt"

$pattern = "^(?<Date>\d{4}-\d{2}-
\d{2})\s+(?<Time>\d{2}:\d{2}:\d{2})\s+ERROR\s+(?<Code>\w+)\s+(
?<Message>.+)$"

foreach ($entry in $logEntries) {

    if ($entry -match $pattern) {

        $date = $matches['Date']

        $time = $matches['Time']

        $code = $matches['Code']

        $message = $matches['Message']

        # Process or store the parsed data

        Write-Host "[$date $time] Code: $code - $message"

    }

}
```

Here,

- **^** and **$** anchor the pattern to the start and end of the line.
- Named capture groups **(?<Date> ...)** and **(?<Time> ...)** isolate specific pieces of data (date, time, error code, message).

The script extracts these values and displays them in a structured format. You could easily convert them to objects and export them to a CSV or JSON file for further analysis.

Working with XML and JSON Data

PowerShell's got your back when it comes to working with structured data formats like XML and JSON. These formats are used a lot for configuration files, data exchange between systems, and interfacing with web services. With the built-in cmdlets and type accelerators, you can easily parse, create, and transform XML and JSON data. This makes it easy to integrate PowerShell with modern APIs and applications.

Processing XML Data

XML (Extensible Markup Language) is a versatile format for storing structured information. In PowerShell, you can work with XML data using the **[xml]** type accelerator, which converts XML content into a manageable object structure.

For example, if you have an XML file named "data.xml", you can load it as follows:

```
[xml]$xmlData = Get-Content -Path "C:\Data\data.xml"
```

Once imported, you can navigate the XML tree using dot notation. Suppose "data.xml" has a structure like this:

```
<Employees>
  <Employee>
    <Name>John Doe</Name>
    <Department>IT</Department>
  </Employee>
  <Employee>
    <Name>Jane Smith</Name>
    <Department>HR</Department>
  </Employee>
</Employees>
```

You can extract the names of all employees by iterating over the nodes:

```
$xmlData.Employees.Employee | ForEach-Object { $_.Name }
```

To search within XML, the **Select-Xml** cmdlet is invaluable. It allows you to query XML using XPath expressions. For instance, to find the employee in the IT department:

```
$itEmployee = Select-Xml -Xml $xmlData -XPath
"//Employee[Department='IT']"
$itEmployee.Node.Name
```

You can also modify XML content by changing node values and then saving the updated XML back to a file using the **Save()** method:

```
$xmlData.Employees.Employee[0].Name = "Jonathan Doe"
```

```
$xmlData.Save("C:\Data\updated_data.xml")
```

This capability makes it easy to automate tasks such as updating configuration files or processing structured data from various sources.

Working with JSON Data

PowerShell offers the **ConvertFrom-Json** and **ConvertTo-Json** cmdlets to convert between JSON strings and PowerShell objects. For example, to convert a JSON string to an object:

```
$jsonString = '{"Name": "Alice", "Department": "Finance"}'
$object = ConvertFrom-Json -InputObject $jsonString
Write-Host "Name: $($object.Name), Department:
$($object.Department)"
```

Once converted, you can manipulate the object like any other PowerShell object. If you need to change a property or add a new one, simply modify it:

```
$object.Location = "Building 5"
```

To convert the modified object back to a JSON string, use:

```
$newJson = $object | ConvertTo-Json -Depth 3
Write-Host $newJson
```

The **-Depth** parameter ensures that nested objects are fully converted. This conversion is useful for sending data to APIs or saving configuration settings in a portable format.

Both XML and JSON processing are of utmost importance in real-world scenarios. For example, consider a scenario where you need to import configuration settings from an XML file, modify them based on business logic, and then export the updated configuration as a JSON file for a web application. You could load the XML, make necessary changes, and then convert the resulting object to JSON:

```
[xml]$configXml = Get-Content -Path "C:\Config\settings.xml"
# Modify configuration (example: update a value)
$configXml.Settings.Timeout = 300
# Convert to a PowerShell object
$configObject = $configXml.Settings
```

```
# Convert the object to JSON
$jsonConfig = $configObject | ConvertTo-Json -Depth 2
# Save the JSON configuration
$jsonConfig | Out-File -FilePath "C:\Config\settings.json"
```

Such workflows facilitate migration between different systems and provide a bridge between legacy XML-based configurations and modern JSON-based applications.

Multithreading and Parallel Processing

Multithreading and parallel processing enable you to execute multiple tasks concurrently, thereby significantly improving performance when dealing with large datasets or time-consuming operations. Rather than processing items sequentially, PowerShell provides several techniques to run tasks in parallel. Here, we will see at some of the approaches to parallel processing, including using the **ForEach-Object -Parallel** parameter, background jobs, and leveraging .NET's threading capabilities.

'ForEach-Object -Parallel'

One of the simplest ways to achieve parallel processing in PowerShell is through the **ForEach-Object -Parallel** parameter, available in PowerShell 7 and above. This method allows you to run a script block for each item in a collection concurrently.

For example, let us look at processing a list of servers to check their disk space:

```
$servers = @("Server1", "Server2", "Server3", "Server4")
$servers | ForEach-Object -Parallel {
    # Simulate a task that takes a random amount of time
    Start-Sleep -Seconds (Get-Random -Minimum 1 -Maximum 5)
    Get-PSDrive -PSProvider FileSystem | Select-Object Name,
@{Name="FreeSpace(MB)";Expression={[math]::Round($_.Free/1MB,2
)}}
} -ThrottleLimit 2
```

In this example, the script block runs in parallel across the servers, with a throttle limit of 2, meaning that at most two tasks run concurrently.

Background Jobs

For scenarios where you need to run tasks asynchronously, PowerShell's background jobs are a powerful alternative. Background jobs allow you to start a task and continue with other operations while the job runs in the background. You can use the **Start-Job** cmdlet to initiate a background job:

```
$job = Start-Job -ScriptBlock {
    # A time-consuming operation, such as processing a large
file
    Get-Content "C:\LargeFile.txt" | Measure-Object -Line
}
```

After starting a job, you can check its status with **Get-Job** and retrieve its output using **Receive-Job**:

```
$job | Wait-Job
$output = Receive-Job -Job $job
Write-Host "Processed lines: $($output.Lines)"
Remove-Job -Job $job
```

Background jobs are particularly useful for decoupling tasks that do not require immediate feedback, allowing you to optimize the overall runtime of your scripts.

Using .NET for Parallel Processing

For more advanced scenarios, you might leverage the .NET Framework's threading capabilities directly from PowerShell. The **[System.Threading.Tasks.Parallel]** class provides methods to run actions concurrently over collections. For example, you can use the **ForEach** method to process items in parallel:

```
$items = 1..10
[System.Threading.Tasks.Parallel]::ForEach($items, {
    param($item)
    Start-Sleep -Seconds (Get-Random -Minimum 1 -Maximum 3)
    Write-Host "Processed item: $item"
})
```

It offers fine-grained control over parallel execution and is particularly effective for CPU-bound tasks.

However, when implementing parallel processing, it is of utmost importance to balance concurrency with system resources. Using too many parallel threads can lead to resource exhaustion, causing performance degradation rather than improvement. The **-ThrottleLimit** parameter in **ForEach-Object -Parallel** allows you to control the maximum number of concurrent threads, enabling you to tailor the level of parallelism to your system's capabilities.

Sample Program: Parallel Data Processing

Imagine you need to process a large collection of log files to extract error messages. Instead of processing them one by one, you can use parallel processing to accelerate the task:

```
$logFiles = Get-ChildItem -Path "C:\Logs" -Filter "*.log"
$errors = $logFiles | ForEach-Object -Parallel {
    param($file)
    # Extract lines containing the word "Error"
    $errorLines = Select-String -Path $file.FullName -Pattern
"Error" | ForEach-Object { $_.Line }
    [PSCustomObject]@{
        FileName = $file.Name
        ErrorCount = $errorLines.Count
        Errors = $errorLines
    }
} -ThrottleLimit 4
$errors | Format-Table -AutoSize
```

This above script processes multiple log files concurrently, extracts error lines, and aggregates the results into a custom object for each file. By using **-ThrottleLimit**, you ensure that no more than four files are processed at once, striking a balance between speed and resource utilization.

Creating Custom Cmdlets and Modules

PowerShell's power lies in its extensibility. One way to extend its functionality is by creating custom cmdlets—specialized commands that encapsulate specific logic. Custom cmdlets allow you to streamline complex operations, integrate with other systems, or enforce business logic that goes beyond what's available through built-in cmdlets.

Building Custom Cmdlets

Custom cmdlets follow the standard Verb-Noun naming convention, making them consistent with the native cmdlets. For example, a cmdlet designed to retrieve detailed system metrics might be named **Get-SystemMetrics**.

One common approach is to write functions in PowerShell that act as cmdlets. Using advanced function parameters and CmdletBinding attributes, you can make these functions behave like native cmdlets.

Let us work around the following example:

```
function Get-HelloWorld {
    [CmdletBinding()]
    param(
        [Parameter(Mandatory = $false)]
        [string]$Name = "World"
    )
    Write-Output "Hello, $Name!"
}
```

This function, **Get-HelloWorld**, uses the CmdletBinding attribute to enable common cmdlet features such as parameter validation and common parameters. By dot-sourcing the script file containing this function, you can test it in your session just like any built-in cmdlet:

```
. .\Get-HelloWorld.ps1
Get-HelloWorld -Name "Alice"
```

From Functions to Modules

Once you have a set of custom functions, you can bundle them into a PowerShell module. Modules are collections of functions, cmdlets, and resources that can be easily imported into any PowerShell session. This modularity helps in organizing your code and sharing it across different projects.

Creating Module Folder

To create a module, first set up a folder with a name matching your module. For example, create a folder named **MyCustomModule**. Inside this folder, place your script file (e.g., **MyCustomModule.psm1**) that contains all your custom functions.

Writing Module File

In **MyCustomModule.psm1**, you include your functions and use the **Export-ModuleMember** cmdlet to specify which functions are exposed:

```
# MyCustomModule.psm1
# Import additional scripts if needed
#. .\Get-HelloWorld.ps1
function Get-HelloWorld {
    [CmdletBinding()]
    param(
        [Parameter(Mandatory = $false)]
        [string]$Name = "World"
    )
    Write-Output "Hello, $Name!"
}
# Export functions to make them available when the module is imported
Export-ModuleMember -Function Get-HelloWorld
```

When this module is imported, only the functions explicitly exported (in this case, **Get-HelloWorld**) will be available in the session.

Creating Module Manifest

Now, to create a manifest for **MyCustomModule**, run the following command in PowerShell within your module folder:

```
New-ModuleManifest -Path .\MyCustomModule.psd1 -RootModule MyCustomModule.psm1 -Author "Your Name" -Description "A module with custom cmdlets for demonstration" -ModuleVersion "1.0"
```

Then edit the resulting **.psd1** file as needed. While you do, ensure that the **FunctionsToExport** field accurately reflects the cmdlets you wish to expose:

```
FunctionsToExport = @('Get-HelloWorld')
```

Importing and Using Module

After creating your module, place the **MyCustomModule** folder in one of the paths specified in the **$env:PSModulePath** environment variable (e.g., **$env:USERPROFILE\Documents\WindowsPowerShell\Modules** for the current user).

You can then import the module in any PowerShell session:

```
Import-Module MyCustomModule
Get-HelloWorld -Name "Bob"
```

This command loads your module, making **Get-HelloWorld** available as a native cmdlet.

For more advanced scenarios, consider developing custom cmdlets using C#. Creating binary modules (.dll files) involves writing a class that derives from **Cmdlet** or **PSCmdlet**, overriding methods like **ProcessRecord()**, and compiling the code with a .NET compiler. While this method is more complex, it offers performance benefits and deep integration with the .NET Framework.

When developing in C#, your code might look like this:

```
using System;
using System.Management.Automation;
[Cmdlet(VerbsCommon.Get, "Greeting")]
public class GetGreetingCmdlet : Cmdlet
{
    [Parameter(Mandatory = false)]
    public string Name { get; set; } = "World";
    protected override void ProcessRecord()
    {
        WriteObject($"Hello, {Name}!");
    }
}
```

After compiling this into a DLL, you create a module manifest that references the binary module. Import it into PowerShell with:

```
Import-Module MyCustomBinaryModule.dll
```

```
Get-Greeting -Name "Alice"
```

By creating custom cmdlets and modules, it empowers you to encapsulate complex logic into simple, easy-to-use commands, which can be shared across teams and environments, and helps in streamlining your administrative workflows.

Using .NET Framework and Assemblies

The PowerShell application is built on the .NET Framework, which provides a rich set of libraries and classes that you can access directly from your scripts. This integration lets you use the full power of .NET for tasks that need more advanced functionality than what's available with native PowerShell cmdlets. So whether you need to work with file systems, handle complex data structures, or create graphical user interfaces, .NET provides a wide range of tools that can enhance your scripts.

Accessing .NET Classes Directly

You can use .NET classes in PowerShell by referring to them with their fully qualified names. For example, to access the **System.IO.File** class for file operations, you can simply call its static methods:

```
$filePath = "C:\Example\test.txt"
$content = [System.IO.File]::ReadAllText($filePath)
Write-Host "File Content: $content"
```

In the above code, **[System.IO.File]::ReadAllText** reads the entire content of the specified file. It allows you to tap into the extensive capabilities of the .NET Framework without having to write additional code in a different language.

Creating .NET Objects

When you need to instantiate a .NET object, you can use the **New-Object** cmdlet or the more modern **::new()** syntax. For instance, to create a new URI object:

```
# Using New-Object
$uri1 = New-Object -TypeName System.Uri -ArgumentList
"https://example.com"
# Using the ::new() syntax
$uri2 = [System.Uri]::new("https://example.com")
```

```
Write-Host "URI: $($uri2.AbsoluteUri)"
```

Both of the methods create an instance of the **System.Uri** class, which you can then use to access various properties and methods.

Accessing Static Members

For many .NET classes, you might only need to access static methods or properties. For example, you can retrieve the current date and time using:

```
$currentDateTime = [System.DateTime]::Now
Write-Host "Current Date and Time: $currentDateTime"
```

This call to **[System.DateTime]::Now** does not require instantiation of a new object; it directly accesses the static property that holds the current system time.

Loading External Assemblies

Sometimes, the functionality you need resides in an external assembly not automatically loaded in your session. You can load these assemblies using the **Add-Type** cmdlet. For example, to load a custom .NET assembly from a DLL file:

```
Add-Type -Path "C:\Path\To\Your\CustomLibrary.dll"
```

Once loaded, you can access the types defined in that assembly just as you would any other .NET class. If the assembly is in the Global Assembly Cache (GAC), you can load it by name:

```
Add-Type -AssemblyName "System.Windows.Forms"
```

Working with .NET Methods and Properties

After loading the necessary assemblies or accessing a .NET class, you can call methods and properties directly. Let us try out an example using the **System.Net.WebClient** class to download a webpage:

```
$webClient = [System.Net.WebClient]::new()
$webClient.Headers.Add("User-Agent", "PowerShell")
$pageContent =
$webClient.DownloadString("https://www.example.com")
Write-Host "Downloaded content length: $($pageContent.Length)"
```

This above script sets up a web client, adds a custom header, downloads the content of the webpage, and then outputs the length of the content.

Using .NET Namespaces

To simplify your scripts, you can import entire .NET namespaces using the **using namespace** directive. This allows you to avoid repeatedly specifying fully qualified class names:

```
using namespace System.IO
$fileInfo = [FileInfo]::new("C:\Example\test.txt")
Write-Host "File Size: $($fileInfo.Length) bytes"
```

With the namespace imported, you can refer to classes like **FileInfo** without prefixing them with **System.IO**, making your code cleaner and easier to read.

Creating Custom .NET Classes

The PowerShell also allows you to define your own .NET classes directly within a script using the **Add-Type** cmdlet with the **-TypeDefinition** parameter. This feature is useful for encapsulating complex logic that may be reused across multiple scripts.

For example:

```
Add-Type -TypeDefinition @"
public class CustomCalculator {
    public static int Add(int a, int b) {
        return a + b;
    }
    public static int Multiply(int a, int b) {
        return a * b;
    }
}
"@
$resultAdd = [CustomCalculator]::Add(5, 3)
$resultMultiply = [CustomCalculator]::Multiply(5, 3)
Write-Host "Sum: $resultAdd, Product: $resultMultiply"
```

This script defines a simple .NET class named **CustomCalculator** with two static methods, **Add** and **Multiply**. Once defined, you can use these methods in your PowerShell scripts to perform calculations or other logic.

Integrating .NET Assemblies

The custom modules can also leverage .NET assemblies to extend their functionality. For example, if you are developing a custom module that requires advanced data processing, you might reference a .NET assembly that provides additional algorithms as below:

```
# MyAdvancedModule.psm1
Add-Type -Path "C:\Libraries\AdvancedProcessing.dll"
function Invoke-AdvancedCalculation {
    param(
        [int]$Number1,
        [int]$Number2
    )
    return
[AdvancedProcessing.Calculator]::Calculate($Number1, $Number2)
}
Export-ModuleMember -Function Invoke-AdvancedCalculation
```

Here, the module demonstrates how you can integrate external .NET functionality into your custom PowerShell modules, thereby extending the capabilities of your scripts.

Summary

Overall, what you took away from this chapter is how to level up your PowerShell scripting skills using some pretty advanced techniques. You learned how to use regular expressions for precise text manipulation, enabling you to search, replace, and extract data with complex patterns. You also checked out ways to work with structured data formats like XML and JSON, which let you integrate with APIs and configuration files without a hitch.

You also discovered multithreading and parallel processing techniques that significantly improved the performance of your scripts by enabling concurrent task execution. You also learned how to create custom cmdlets and modules, which help encapsulate complex logic into reusable components. Finally, you became proficient at integrating the .NET Framework and assemblies into your PowerShell scripts to take advantage of rich libraries and advanced functionality.

CHAPTER 14: POWERSHELL AND AUTOMATION FRAMEWORKS

Chapter Overview

This chapter introduces you to the integration of PowerShell with modern automation frameworks. You will explore and get hands-on with how these frameworks will provide a structured approach to organizing and managing your scripts, enforcing best practices, and supporting complex workflows such as continuous integration and continuous deployment. You will learn to leverage Ansible, Chef, and Puppet to automate the configuration and management of diverse environments across Windows and Linux systems.

Furthermore, you will practically learn to integrate PowerShell into your CI/CD pipelines with Jenkins and Azure DevOps. You will learn to combine the flexibility of PowerShell scripting to create end-to-end automation workflows that streamline build, test, and deployment processes. By the end, you will will be well thorough with the practical strategies and tools necessary to create and manage automated, cross-platform workflows for operational efficiency and agility.

Introduction to Automation Frameworks

In today's IT landscape, automation frameworks have become indispensable, enabling organizations to streamline the management of their infrastructure, applications, and services. These frameworks provide standardized ways of doing things, libraries, and tools that make the automation process easier. This ensures that tasks are done the same way every time and without any problems. Here we explore the basic concepts of automation frameworks and examine how they increase productivity, reduce errors, and support continuous integration and deployment in modern environments.

Role of Automation Frameworks

Automation frameworks serve several critical functions within an organization:

- They offer a structured approach for organizing scripts, often by encapsulating reusable functions, cmdlets, and modules into well-defined packages. This structure not only makes it easier to maintain scripts over time but also ensures that best practices are consistently followed.
- Frameworks enforce coding standards and naming conventions. By adhering to these guidelines, IT teams ensure that scripts are more readable, maintainable, and less prone to errors. Standardization also helps prevent configuration drift, which is the gradual deviation of system settings from a defined baseline.
- Complex business processes and IT operations, such as application deployment, configuration management, and system monitoring, benefit greatly from automation frameworks. These tools orchestrate tasks across multiple systems, ensuring that every step in the process is executed in the correct sequence.
- Many frameworks include built-in testing mechanisms that allow you to validate

configurations before they are applied. Unit testing, integration testing, and acceptance testing are integral to ensuring that scripts perform as expected in production environments.

- Automation frameworks integrate seamlessly with CI/CD tools. They enable teams to automate the entire lifecycle—from code check-in and testing to deployment and monitoring—thus accelerating release cycles and enhancing overall operational efficiency.
- Modern frameworks, especially with the advent of PowerShell Core, support cross-platform environments. This means that the same automation logic can be applied across Windows, Linux, and macOS systems, providing a unified approach to system management.

Essential Components

There are several core components underpin effective automation frameworks:

- Libraries and Modules

These contain reusable code that can be imported into scripts. They often include functions for common tasks like file management, network operations, and system monitoring.

- Configuration Management Tools

There are tools like PowerShell DSC and other configuration management systems that ensure systems remain in a desired state. It helps in reducing the need for manual intervention.

- Testing Tools

The automation frameworks often integrate with testing tools such as Pester for PowerShell. These tools enable you to run tests on your scripts, ensuring that they work as expected before deployment.

- Orchestration and Workflow Engines

These components help coordinate multiple tasks and processes, ensuring that each task is executed in the correct order and that dependencies are managed appropriately.

- Version Control Integration

The automation scripts are stored in version control systems (such as Git) to ensure that changes are tracked over time, enabling collaboration and rollback when needed.

The integration of automation frameworks in IT operations provides numerous benefits:

- By automating repetitive tasks, administrators can focus on more strategic initiatives. Automation frameworks reduce manual workload and accelerate routine operations.
- Automated processes are less prone to the mistakes that can occur with manual intervention. This consistency ensures that configurations remain aligned with

organizational standards.

- Automation enables rapid deployment of updates, applications, and configurations. In the event of an issue, rollback procedures can be implemented quickly and reliably.
- With standardized scripts and automated logging, organizations can easily meet regulatory requirements and internal policies. Auditing becomes simpler, as the execution of tasks is consistently recorded and monitored.
- Automation frameworks are designed to handle large-scale environments. Whether you are managing a few servers or thousands of devices, these frameworks allow for seamless scaling of operations.

So imagine you've got this super important update to push out to a bunch of servers, maybe even hundreds. An automation framework lets you write a single script that deploys the update and also validates the configuration, logs each action, and reports on the deployment status. This way, you don't have to do the same tasks over and over, and you can be sure that all your systems are updated the same way.

Another example is when you're dealing with complex workflows, like setting up new virtual machines, configuring network settings, and deploying applications—all with one script. These frameworks help you tie all these tasks together, making sure each step is done successfully before moving on to the next. This reduces downtime and increases efficiency.

PowerShell and Ansible

Ansible is a powerful, open-source automation tool that excels in configuration management, application deployment, and orchestration. Unlike traditional scripting methods, Ansible uses a simple, human-readable language (YAML) to define tasks and workflows. When integrated with PowerShell, Ansible extends its automation capabilities to Windows environments, bridging the gap between Linux-based automation and Windows administration.

Why Integrate Ansible?

There are a few good reasons why Ansible is integrated with PowerShell.

- Ansible is usually used in Linux environments, but by combining it with PowerShell, you can manage Windows hosts more efficiently. This makes it so you can automate things the same way across different IT environments.
- Ansible's agentless architecture, which uses SSH or WinRM for communication, makes configuration management a breeze. When you pair Ansible with PowerShell's strong scripting skills, you can automate complex Windows tasks with minimal overhead.
- Ansible is designed to scale. Whether you're handling a few machines or thousands, Ansible's playbooks let you run tasks at the same time, cutting down on manual effort and boosting efficiency.
- Ansible uses a declarative language to define the desired state of your systems. It works

well with PowerShell DSC and other configuration management tools, making it easier to create a more consistent and standard automation strategy.

A lot of organizations already use Ansible for Linux automation. Now that Ansible can also work with Windows using PowerShell, you can use the same playbooks, inventory files, and orchestration tools, which makes your automation processes more consistent.

Configuring Ansible

Before you can use Ansible to manage Windows hosts, several prerequisites must be met:

- Typically, Ansible runs on a Linux control node. However, it can also run on Windows using the Windows Subsystem for Linux (WSL). Ensure that Ansible is installed and properly configured on your control node.
- Windows Remote Management (WinRM) must be enabled and configured on all target Windows machines. This involves setting up WinRM listeners and ensuring that appropriate firewall rules are in place. Secure WinRM configurations often include using HTTPS and strong authentication methods.

Create an inventory file (e.g., **`/etc/ansible/hosts`**) that lists your Windows hosts. Then specify connection details using parameters such as **`ansible_connection`**, **`ansible_user`**, **`ansible_password`**, and **`ansible_winrm_transport`**.

A sample inventory entry might look like this:

```
[windows]
winhost1.example.com
[windows:vars]
ansible_connection=winrm
ansible_user=Administrator
ansible_password=YourPassword
ansible_winrm_server_cert_validation=ignore
ansible_winrm_transport=ntlm
```

Using Ansible Modules

The Ansible provides several Windows-specific modules that leverage PowerShell under the hood. These modules allow you to manage files, services, packages, and more on Windows hosts. For example, the **`win_shell`** module executes PowerShell commands on a remote Windows machine.

Try to work on the below simple playbook example:

```
---
- name: Execute PowerShell commands on Windows hosts
  hosts: windows
  tasks:
    - name: Retrieve disk information
      win_shell: Get-PSDrive -PSProvider FileSystem |
ConvertTo-Json
      register: disk_info
    - name: Display disk information
      debug:
        var: disk_info.stdout | from_json
```

In this playbook:

- The **win_shell** module runs a PowerShell command that retrieves disk drive information and converts it to JSON.
- The output is then registered and processed using the **debug** module to display the information in a structured format.

Combining PowerShell and Ansible

You can use Ansible playbooks to do complex admin tasks on Windows hosts by adding multiple modules and custom scripts. For example, you could design a playbook that deploys a new application, configures system settings, and verifies the installation using PowerShell commands.

Following is a quick example to get you started:

```
---
- name: Deploy and Configure Application on Windows
  hosts: windows
  tasks:
    - name: Create a directory for the application
      win_file:
        path: C:\Application
        state: directory
    - name: Deploy application files
```

```
    win_copy:
      src: /path/to/local/app/
      dest: C:\Application\
      recurse: yes
  - name: Configure application settings using PowerShell
    win_shell: |
      Set-ItemProperty -Path "C:\Application\config.ini" -
Name "AppMode" -Value "Production"
    register: config_result
  - name: Verify configuration
    win_shell: |
      (Get-ItemProperty -Path
"C:\Application\config.ini").AppMode
    register: verify_result
  - name: Display configuration result
    debug:
      msg: "Application mode is set to {{
verify_result.stdout }}"
```

This above playbook performs several tasks:

- Creates the necessary directory on the target Windows host.
- Copies application files from the control node to the target machine.
- Runs a PowerShell command to update configuration settings.
- Verifies that the settings have been applied.
- Outputs the configuration result for confirmation.

So, when you combine Ansible with PowerShell, you can use the strengths of both tools to manage Windows environments effectively. This combo not only makes configuration and deployment tasks easier, but it also makes overall system management and operational consistency better.

PowerShell and Chef

Chef is a robust configuration management tool designed to automate the deployment, configuration, and management of infrastructure. When integrated with PowerShell, Chef extends its powerful automation capabilities to Windows environments, allowing you to leverage PowerShell's rich scripting language alongside Chef's declarative configuration models. This integration provides a cohesive workflow where you can manage Windows hosts using Chef cookbooks that include PowerShell scripts for tasks such as application deployment, system configuration, and service management.

Now before diving into the integration, it's important to make sure your environment is set up properly.

- First, you'll need to install Chef Workstation on your local machine. This gives you tools like knife and the Chef Development Kit (DK), which are essential for creating and managing cookbooks.
- Set up a Chef Server that will be the main place for your cookbooks and node configurations.
- Make sure your Windows nodes have the Chef Client installed and are configured to communicate with your Chef Server. Proper network connectivity and security configurations (like firewall rules) must be in place.
- Make sure PowerShell is installed and updated on all Windows nodes, and that any necessary modules (e.g., ActiveDirectory, WebAdministration) are available.
- And finally, make sure you've got a secure way to manage your credentials, like using Windows Credential Manager or encrypted data bags in Chef. This keeps your sensitive data safe and secure in your cookbooks or scripts.

Creating Chef Cookbook

The Chef cookbooks are the primary building blocks for configuring nodes with Chef. Now, to integrate PowerShell into your configuration management process, create a new cookbook that includes PowerShell recipes.

Now, start to begin by generating a cookbook using Chef Workstation's command-line tools:

```
chef generate cookbook powershell_example
```

This command creates a directory named **`powershell_example`** with a standard structure, including directories for recipes, attributes, templates, and more.

Once the cookbook is generated, you can start editing the recipes to incorporate PowerShell commands.

Integrating PowerShell

Chef provides the **`powershell_script`** resource, which is specifically designed for executing PowerShell commands on Windows nodes. This resource enables you to embed PowerShell code directly into your Chef recipes. For example, to create a recipe that retrieves disk information and writes it to a file, your recipe (e.g., **`recipes/run_powershell.rb`**) might look like this:

```
powershell_script 'Get Disk Information' do
  code <<-EOH
    $diskInfo = Get-PSDrive -PSProvider FileSystem |
ConvertTo-Json
    Set-Content -Path 'C:\\Logs\\DiskInfo.json' -Value
$diskInfo
  EOH
  guard_interpreter :powershell_script
  not_if '(Test-Path "C:\\Logs\\DiskInfo.json")'
end
```

In this example:

- The **powershell_script** resource executes the PowerShell code enclosed within the HEREDOC syntax.
- The script gathers disk drive information and converts it to JSON before saving it to a file.
- The **not_if** guard ensures that the script does not run if the log file already exists.

Deploying and Managing PowerShell Scripts

Once your cookbook is ready, you need to deploy it to your Windows nodes. You can use Chef's **knife** command-line tool to upload the cookbook to the Chef Server:

```
knife cookbook upload powershell_example
```

After uploading, assign the cookbook to the desired nodes by adding the appropriate recipe to the node's run-list. For example:

```
knife node run_list add "windows-node.example.com"
"recipe[powershell_example::run_powershell]"
```

When the Chef Client runs on the Windows node (either manually or via scheduled runs), it will execute the recipes in the run-list, including those that run PowerShell scripts.

In addition to simple script execution, you can leverage Chef to handle more complex PowerShell workflows. For instance, you can design recipes that handle conditional logic, interact with external APIs, or integrate with other Windows management tools. Consider a scenario where you need to update configuration settings across multiple servers. You could create a recipe that uses PowerShell to modify registry settings or update configuration files, then validate the changes using Chef's built-in resources.

Another advanced use case involves handling error conditions. By combining PowerShell's robust error handling (using try-catch blocks) with Chef's notification and logging features, you can ensure that any issues during script execution are promptly reported and addressed. This dual-layer approach enhances both automation reliability and security.

PowerShell and Puppet

Puppet's a pretty powerful configuration management tool that automates the deployment and management of infrastructure. It's usually used in Linux environments, but it also works with Windows thanks to its agent-based model. And when you combine Puppet with PowerShell, you get the best of both worlds. Puppet's straightforward, reusable configurations and PowerShell's advanced scripting features for specific Windows tasks. The integration streamlines management tasks, ensures consistency across your infrastructure, and reduces manual intervention.

Creating Puppet Module

Puppet modules are the building blocks of configuration management in Puppet. To integrate PowerShell, create a new module that includes Puppet manifests designed to execute PowerShell scripts. Start by generating a new module using the Puppet Development Kit:

```
pdk new module powershell_example --skip-interview
```

This command creates a new module named **powershell_example** with a standard structure, including directories for manifests, files, templates, and tests. You can now develop your manifests to incorporate PowerShell tasks.

Writing Puppet Manifests

Now here, within your Puppet module, create a manifest (for example, **manifests/run_powershell.pp**) that leverages the **exec** resource to run PowerShell commands. The **exec** resource in Puppet allows you to execute arbitrary commands on the target system. To execute a PowerShell script, specify the command with the appropriate syntax:

```
class powershell_example::run_powershell {
  exec { 'Run PowerShell Script':
    command   => 'powershell.exe -NoProfile -ExecutionPolicy
Bypass -File "C:\\path\\to\\script.ps1"',
    provider  => 'powershell',
    cwd       => 'C:\\',
```

```
    timeout    => 300,
    logoutput => true,
  }
}
```

In this above manifest,

- **command** specifies the PowerShell executable and the script to run.
- **provider** ensures that the command is executed using the PowerShell provider.
- **cwd** sets the current working directory.
- **timeout** limits the execution time to prevent long-running or hung processes.
- **logoutput** enables logging of the command's output, which is useful for debugging.

This manifest encapsulates the process of executing a PowerShell script as part of your Puppet configuration.

Integrating PowerShell Output

Often, you may need to capture the output of a PowerShell script and use it within your Puppet manifests. Puppet can parse and act upon this output, enabling dynamic configuration based on real-time data. For example, consider a scenario where you need to determine system information using PowerShell and then configure the node accordingly. Although Puppet's native capabilities for parsing command output are limited compared to PowerShell, you can use facts or external scripts to integrate this data. One approach is to have a PowerShell script output JSON data, then use a custom fact in Puppet to process that information:

PowerShell Script:

```
$systemInfo = @{
  OSVersion = (Get-CimInstance Win32_OperatingSystem).Version
  Memory    = (Get-CimInstance
Win32_ComputerSystem).TotalPhysicalMemory
}
$systemInfo | ConvertTo-Json
Custom Puppet Fact (using Facter):
Facter.add('system_info') do
  setcode do
```

```
    output = Facter::Util::Resolution.exec('powershell.exe -
NoProfile -ExecutionPolicy Bypass -File
"C:\\path\\to\\system_info.ps1"')
    JSON.parse(output) rescue {}
  end
end
```

This integration allows you to dynamically tailor your configuration based on the current state of the node, with PowerShell providing the detailed data and Puppet acting on that information.

Integrating PowerShell with CI/CD Tools

PowerShell's integration with Continuous Integration and Continuous Deployment (CI/CD) tools is a game-changer for IT teams. It allows them to automate the build, test, and deployment processes across environments with ease. This integration lets you use PowerShell's strong scripting abilities to handle Windows-specific tasks while using CI/CD pipelines to manage workflows across different stages of software delivery. This combination makes for more reliable, repeatable, and scalable deployments, and it reduces manual intervention and accelerates release cycles.

PowerShell provides extensive support for automation and configuration management, and when integrated with CI/CD tools like Jenkins, Azure DevOps, or GitLab CI/CD, it becomes an even more potent asset.

Some of the main benefits are:

- First, when you automate the whole lifecycle—from code commit to production deployment—you make sure that all changes are tested and validated before they reach end users.
- You can also use scripts to handle things like environment configuration, software installation, and system updates. These scripts can be integrated into pipelines, which reduces repetitive manual tasks.
- Automated deployments make sure each environment is configured just how it should be, which prevents configuration drift and improves stability.
- CI/CD pipelines provide immediate feedback on code quality and deployment success, enabling teams to quickly identify and fix issues.

Integrating with Jenkins

Jenkins is one of the most popular open-source CI/CD tools and provides excellent support for running PowerShell scripts on Windows environments. Here’s how you can integrate PowerShell into a Jenkins pipeline:

Installing PowerShell Plugin

In your Jenkins dashboard, navigate to "Manage Jenkins" > "Manage Plugins." Under the "Available" tab, search for "PowerShell" and install the plugin. This plugin enables you to add PowerShell build steps in your Jenkins jobs.

Creating Jenkins Job

Create a new Jenkins job (Freestyle project or Pipeline project) and configure the source code repository from which your PowerShell scripts will be pulled. In a Pipeline job, you can define a Jenkinsfile that outlines the stages of your CI/CD process.

Defining Pipeline

In your Jenkinsfile, you need to add a stage to run PowerShell scripts. For example, a simple Jenkinsfile might look like this:

```
pipeline {
    agent any
    stages {
        stage('Build') {
            steps {
                powershell '''
                    # Build your project using PowerShell
                    Write-Host "Building the project..."
                    # Your build commands here
                '''
            }
        }
        stage('Test') {
            steps {
                powershell '''
                    Write-Host "Running tests..."
                    # Execute your test scripts here
                '''
            }
```

```
        }
        stage('Deploy') {
            steps {
                powershell '''
                    Write-Host "Deploying the application..."
                    # Deployment scripts, for example:
                    # Invoke-Command -ComputerName
"ProdServer" -ScriptBlock { <deployment commands> }
                '''
            }
        }
    }
}
```

This Pipeline demonstrates how to incorporate multiple stages (build, test, deploy) with PowerShell commands at each stage. You can expand each section with more detailed scripts based on your requirements.

Integrating with Azure DevOps

Azure DevOps provides a cloud-based CI/CD platform that integrates naturally with PowerShell. You can add PowerShell tasks to your build and release pipelines, allowing you to automate various aspects of deployment and configuration management.

Now to integrate, in your Azure Pipelines, add tasks that run PowerShell scripts. These tasks can include inline scripts or reference script files stored in your repository. A sample Azure Pipeline YAML file may include steps like:

```
trigger:
  branches:
    include:
      - main
pool:
  vmImage: 'windows-latest'
steps:
```

```
- task: PowerShell@2
  inputs:
    targetType: 'inline'
    script: |
      Write-Host "Starting build process..."
      # Insert build commands here
- task: PowerShell@2
  inputs:
    targetType: 'filePath'
    filePath: 'scripts/deploy.ps1'
```

This YAML configuration kicks off a pipeline when the main branch changes, runs an inline PowerShell script for the build stage, and executes an external deployment script.

The combo of PowerShell's flexibility with the orchestration prowess of CI/CD platforms leads to faster, more reliable deployments and cuts down on the manual overhead of handling complicated IT setups - which is pretty sweet!

Summary

To sum it up, this short chapter was all about how to use PowerShell with modern automation frameworks to improve IT operations. You saw how these frameworks give you a step-by-step process for organizing scripts and automating processes. They also make sure that everything is done properly and securely. To streamline deployments, manage configurations, and generate reports, you explored how PowerShell integrates with tools such as Ansible, Chef, Pusppet, and CI/CD platforms such as Jenkins and Azure DevOps. With these integrations, you can automate complex workflows across different environments, ensure consistency, reduce manual errors, and improve the efficiency of IT operations.

Chapter 15: Extending PowerShell and Interoperability

Chapter Overview

In this chapter, you will explore to enhance and extend PowerShell beyond its built-in capabilities. You will learn to create custom functions, modules, cmdlets, and even classes, which allow you to encapsulate and reuse sophisticated logic tailored to your environment. By building these extensions, you can overcome limitations of native commands and address specific operational challenges, ensuring your scripts are both powerful and adaptable. It covers various methods for extending PowerShell, including writing custom cmdlets in PowerShell or a .NET language, developing reusable modules, and leveraging object-oriented programming to create custom classes.

Additionally, you will examine PowerShell's interoperability, wherein you will see how PowerShell can interact with RESTful APIs, call external scripts written in Python and Bash, and work with other automation tools to create a unified workflow across diverse environments. You will learn how these integrations help bridge gaps between different systems and enhance the overall automation strategy.

Extending PowerShell

To extend PowerShell is to extend its native capabilities to meet unique business needs. You can build custom functions, modules, and cmdlets to tailor PowerShell to specific tasks in your environment. This makes PowerShell go from being a general-purpose shell to a powerful, domain-specific tool that can put complex business logic into reusable components.

Custom Functions and Advanced Scripting

One of the simplest ways to extend PowerShell is by writing custom functions. These functions allow you to abstract repetitive or complex operations into a single command. You can design functions that accept parameters, process pipeline input, and return structured objects. For example, you might create a function that aggregates server metrics from multiple sources and returns a detailed report.

Parameterization and Validation

Leverage PowerShell's advanced parameter attributes such as **`[Parameter()]`**, **`[ValidateNotNullOrEmpty()]`**, and **`[ValidateSet()]`** to ensure your functions accept valid input. This not only improves reliability but also prevents misuse.

Pipeline Support

By designing functions to accept pipeline input, you can integrate your custom functions seamlessly with other cmdlets. This promotes reusability and the development of sophisticated one-liners that combine multiple operations into a single command.

Building Modules

Modules are collections of functions, cmdlets, and related resources. They help you organize your custom code, making it easier to maintain, share, and reuse. Creating a module involves:

- Module Structure

You must organize your code into a folder with a meaningful name (e.g., **MyExtendedTools**). Inside, place your script file(s) (typically with a ***.psm1*** extension) that contain your custom functions.

- Module Manifest

A manifest (**.psd1** file) provides metadata about the module, such as the version, author, and list of exported functions. You can use the **New-ModuleManifest** cmdlet to create one. For example:

```
New-ModuleManifest -Path
"C:\MyExtendedTools\MyExtendedTools.psd1" -RootModule
MyExtendedTools.psm1 -Author "Your Name" -Description "A
module with custom extended functionalities for PowerShell" -
ModuleVersion "1.0"
```

- Exporting Members

In your module script, use the **Export-ModuleMember** cmdlet to expose specific functions. This practice keeps your module interface clean and controlled, ensuring that only the necessary components are available to end users.

Developing Custom Cmdlets

For more advanced functionality or better performance, you may choose to create custom cmdlets using a .NET language like C#. Custom cmdlets are compiled into binary modules (DLLs) and integrate deeply with the PowerShell engine. The process includes:

- Writing Cmdlet

Create a class that inherits from the **Cmdlet** or **PSCmdlet** base class. Override methods such as **BeginProcessing()**, **ProcessRecord()**, and **EndProcessing()** to implement your logic. This gives you full control over how the cmdlet processes input and produces output.

- Compiling and Packaging

Use Visual Studio or the .NET CLI to compile your code into a DLL. Once compiled, create a module manifest that references your binary module and import it into PowerShell using **Import-Module**.

- Integration and Testing

Be sure to test your custom cmdlets thoroughly to ensure that they work as intended. Custom cmdlets are great because they're really fast and work well with .NET functionalities. They're perfect for high-performance or complex operations.

PowerShell Classes

With PowerShell 5.0 and later, you can define classes directly within your scripts. This introduces object-oriented programming to your automation tasks, enabling you to create complex data structures and reusable components.

Defining Classes

Use the **class** keyword to define a new class. For example, a class that encapsulates server configuration might include properties for hostname, IP address, and role, along with methods for validation or reporting.

```
class ServerConfiguration {
    [string]$Hostname
    [string]$IPAddress
    [string]$Role
    ServerConfiguration([string]$hostname, [string]$ip,
[string]$role) {
        $this.Hostname = $hostname
        $this.IPAddress = $ip
        $this.Role = $role
    }
    [string] GetSummary() {
        return "Server: $($this.Hostname) | IP:
$($this.IPAddress) | Role: $($this.Role)"
    }
}
```

Creating and Using Class Instances

Once defined, you can create instances of your classes and call their methods. This object-oriented approach enhances code clarity and reusability.

```
$server = [ServerConfiguration]::new("Server01",
"192.168.1.10", "Web Server")
Write-Host $server.GetSummary()
```

By enhancing PowerShell with custom functions, modules, cmdlets, and classes, you can create a customized automation environment that meets your specific needs. This flexibility not only boosts your productivity but also makes sure your scripts stay easy to maintain, scalable, and secure over time.

Interoperability

The concept of interoperability refers to its ability to work seamlessly with a wide range of tools, technologies, and platforms. This capability is a key factor behind PowerShell's popularity, as it allows administrators to integrate diverse systems—from Windows and Linux environments to cloud services and third-party APIs—using a single, unified scripting language.

Cross-Platform Support with PowerShell Core

PowerShell Core, built on .NET Core, is inherently cross-platform. Unlike the Windows-only version, PowerShell Core runs on Windows, Linux, and macOS. This cross-platform capability means that the same scripts can manage systems across different operating systems.

Installation and Compatibility

Installing PowerShell Core on various platforms is straightforward, with packages available for most distributions. Once installed, you can run your PowerShell scripts on any supported platform, making it easier to manage heterogeneous environments.

Unified Scripting Language

With PowerShell Core, you can write scripts that include conditional logic, loops, and advanced functions that work consistently regardless of the underlying operating system. This unification reduces the learning curve and simplifies administration across different platforms.

RESTful APIs and Web Services

PowerShell's ability to interact with RESTful APIs greatly enhances its interoperability. Using cmdlets like **`Invoke-RestMethod`** and **`Invoke-WebRequest`**, you can send HTTP requests, receive responses, and process data in formats like JSON or XML.

Integrating with Cloud Services

Many cloud platforms, such as Azure, AWS, and Google Cloud, provide RESTful APIs.

PowerShell enables you to manage cloud resources by making API calls. For example, using the Azure PowerShell module, you can automate the creation of virtual machines, manage storage accounts, and configure network settings seamlessly.

Interacting with Third-Party Services

Whether you need to retrieve data from a public API or interact with a custom web service, PowerShell makes it easy. You can convert JSON responses into PowerShell objects for further processing, ensuring that your scripts can adapt to various data formats and protocols.

Integration with Scripting Languages

PowerShell can interact with other scripting languages, providing a bridge between different automation tools.

Integrating with Python

By calling Python scripts from within PowerShell, you can leverage Python's rich ecosystem of libraries for tasks such as data analysis or machine learning. You can use the **&** operator or **Start-Process** to execute Python scripts and capture their output.

```
$pythonPath = "C:\Python39\python.exe"
$scriptPath = ".\my_python_script.py"
$result = & $pythonPath $scriptPath 5 7
Write-Host "Result from Python: $result"
```

Integrating with Bash

In cross-platform environments, especially with PowerShell Core, you can invoke Bash scripts. This is particularly useful when working on systems that have both PowerShell and Bash available (e.g., Windows with WSL, Linux, or macOS).

```
$bashPath = "wsl"
$bashScript = "/mnt/c/path/to/my_bash_script.sh"
$result = & $bashPath $bashScript 5 7
Write-Host "Result from Bash: $result"
```

When you focus on interoperability, you unlock the full potential of PowerShell to serve as a bridge between disparate systems and technologies. This integration makes automation more efficient and lets your organization adapt quickly to changing IT landscapes and new platforms.

Integrating PowerShell with Python and Bash

You can use PowerShell with other scripting languages like Python and Bash to make your automation toolkit more versatile. You can combine these languages and use each one's strengths: PowerShell's tight integration with Windows and its strong object-oriented features, Python's extensive ecosystem for data manipulation and scientific computing, and Bash's lightweight efficiency on Unix-like systems. This means you can create hybrid scripts that handle tasks more effectively than any single language could on its own.

Integrating PowerShell with Python

Python is widely known for its simplicity, readability, and extensive library support. It excels at tasks like data analysis, machine learning, and interacting with various web APIs. Integrating Python with PowerShell allows you to call Python scripts from within your PowerShell environment, thus combining Windows administration with powerful data processing capabilities.

Calling Python Scripts

You can invoke Python scripts from PowerShell using the call operator (**&**) or the **Start-Process** cmdlet. Here's a simple example:

First, create a file named **my_python_script.py** with the following content:

```
import sys
def add_numbers(a, b):
    return a + b
if __name__ == "__main__":
    num1 = int(sys.argv[1])
    num2 = int(sys.argv[2])
    result = add_numbers(num1, num2)
    print(result)
```

Next, in PowerShell, execute the Python script and capture its output:

```
$pythonPath = "C:\Python39\python.exe"  # Adjust the path as
necessary
$scriptPath = "C:\Path\To\my_python_script.py"
$num1 = 5
$num2 = 7
```

```
$result = & $pythonPath $scriptPath $num1 $num2
Write-Host "The result from Python is: $result"
```

This example demonstrates how you can pass arguments from PowerShell to a Python script and process the output seamlessly.

Handling Complex Data Exchange

For more advanced scenarios, you might need to exchange complex data between PowerShell and Python. One effective method is to use JSON as a common data format. For this, first convert a PowerShell object to JSON and pass it as an argument to the Python script.

```
$data = @{ name = "Alice"; age = 30 }
$jsonData = $data | ConvertTo-Json -Compress
$result = & $pythonPath $scriptPath $jsonData
```

In your Python script, parse the JSON input using Python's **json** module, process it, and output the result as JSON. PowerShell can then convert the JSON output back into an object using **ConvertFrom-Json**.

This technique ensures a structured, language-agnostic means of data exchange, allowing both environments to process complex data sets efficiently.

Integrating PowerShell with Bash

Bash is the default shell on many Unix-like systems, and its lightweight scripting capabilities make it ideal for tasks like file manipulation, system monitoring, and text processing. Integrating Bash with PowerShell enables you to run Bash commands and scripts from within a PowerShell session—especially useful on Windows systems with Windows Subsystem for Linux (WSL) or in cross-platform environments using PowerShell Core.

Setting up Bash Integration

If you are on a Windows system, ensure that you have WSL installed and configured. You can install WSL by running:

```
wsl --install
```

Alternatively, on Linux or macOS, Bash is typically available by default.

Calling Bash Scripts

You can invoke Bash scripts using the call operator (**&**) or the **Start-Process** cmdlet. For this, create a file named **my_bash_script.sh** with the following content:

```
#!/bin/bash
function add_numbers() {
    echo $(($1 + $2))
}
num1=$1
num2=$2
result=$(add_numbers $num1 $num2)
echo $result
 Make the script executable:
chmod +x my_bash_script.sh
Invoke the Bash Script from PowerShell:
On a Windows system with WSL, you can call the Bash script
like this:
$bashPath = "wsl"
$bashScript = "/mnt/c/Path/To/my_bash_script.sh"
$num1 = 5
$num2 = 7
$result = & $bashPath $bashScript $num1 $num2
Write-Host "The result from Bash is: $result"
```

On Linux or macOS, simply use the Bash executable path (e.g., **/bin/bash**).

Advanced Integration Techniques

For scenarios where more complex interactions are required, you might combine the outputs of Bash scripts with PowerShell processing. For instance, if your Bash script outputs a multi-line result, you can capture and process each line in PowerShell:

```
$result = & $bashPath $bashScript $num1 $num2
$resultArray = $result -split "`n"
foreach ($line in $resultArray) {
    Write-Host "Output: $line"
```

```
}
```

It allows you to handle structured output from Bash and incorporate it into larger PowerShell workflows. Whether you need Python's extensive libraries for data analytics or Bash's efficiency for system-level tasks, combining these tools in a unified automation script enhances your flexibility and productivity.

PowerShell and RESTful APIs

The RESTful APIs are a cornerstone of modern application development, enabling communication between disparate systems over HTTP. PowerShell, with its native support for HTTP requests, provides robust tools for interacting with these APIs. Using cmdlets like **Invoke-RestMethod** and **Invoke-WebRequest**, you can send and receive data in JSON or XML formats, integrate with cloud services, and automate tasks that require remote service interaction.

Using Invoke-RestMethod

The **Invoke-RestMethod** is designed for interacting with RESTful APIs by simplifying the process of making HTTP requests and automatically converting JSON or XML responses into PowerShell objects.

So here, to retrieve data from an API, you can use a simple GET request. For example:

```
$apiUrl = "https://api.example.com/users"
$response = Invoke-RestMethod -Uri $apiUrl -Method Get
foreach ($user in $response) {
    Write-Host "User ID: $($user.id), Name: $($user.name)"
}
```

This command fetches data from the API, and PowerShell automatically converts the JSON response into objects that can be easily iterated over.

Now, when you need to send data to an API, you can construct a JSON payload and use the POST method:

```
$apiUrl = "https://api.example.com/users"
$newUser = @{
    name  = "John Doe"
```

```
    email = "john.doe@example.com"
}
$jsonBody = $newUser | ConvertTo-Json
$response = Invoke-RestMethod -Uri $apiUrl -Method Post -
ContentType "application/json" -Body $jsonBody
Write-Host "Response: $response"
```

This sends the new user data to the API and displays the response.

Using Invoke-WebRequest

For scenarios requiring more control over HTTP requests and responses, **Invoke-WebRequest** offers additional features, such as detailed response headers and status codes. So, to make a GET request and handle the response manually, use:

```
$apiUrl = "https://api.example.com/users"
$response = Invoke-WebRequest -Uri $apiUrl -Method Get
$content = $response.Content | ConvertFrom-Json
foreach ($user in $content) {
    Write-Host "User ID: $($user.id), Name: $($user.name)"
}
```

When working with APIs that require custom headers or authentication tokens, **Invoke-WebRequest** can be configured accordingly:

```
$apiUrl = "https://api.example.com/users"
$headers = @{
    "Authorization" = "Bearer YourAccessToken"
}
$newUser = @{
    name  = "Jane Doe"
    email = "jane.doe@example.com"
}
$jsonBody = $newUser | ConvertTo-Json
```

```
$response = Invoke-WebRequest -Uri $apiUrl -Method Post -
Headers $headers -ContentType "application/json" -Body
$jsonBody

Write-Host "Response Code: $($response.StatusCode)"
```

This example demonstrates to include authentication headers in your request, which is common in secured API environments.

Handling Complex Data and Errors

When dealing with RESTful APIs, error handling and data validation are of much need and must be done carefully. We need to wrap your API calls in try-catch blocks to handle exceptions gracefully:

```
try {

    $response = Invoke-RestMethod -Uri
"https://api.example.com/data" -Method Get -ErrorAction Stop

    Write-Host "Data retrieved successfully."

} catch {

    Write-Warning "Failed to retrieve data: $_"

}
```

Additionally, you may need to process large datasets or paginate results from an API.

Integrating API Data into Workflows

The true power of RESTful API integration lies in using API data to drive automation. For instance, you might query an API to obtain the latest software version, then use that information to trigger an update process on your servers.

```
$apiUrl = "https://api.example.com/software/latest"

$latestVersion = Invoke-RestMethod -Uri $apiUrl -Method Get

if ($latestVersion -ne $currentVersion) {

    Write-Host "A new version is available. Initiating
update..."

    # Call update script or perform deployment tasks

} else {
```

```
    Write-Host "Software is up to date."
}
```

Overall, by leveraging **Invoke-RestMethod** and **Invoke-WebRequest**, you can easily send and receive data from web services, integrate with cloud platforms, and create responsive, data-driven scripts.

Creating and Consuming Web Services

As the automation and integration of business processes increases, the creation and consumption of Web services becomes an essential skill. The PowerShell enables you to quickly set up simple web services using native .NET capabilities and consume them seamlessly within your scripts. This empowers you to build custom APIs, integrate disparate systems, and facilitate communication between applications. In this section, you will learn how to create a basic web service using PowerShell and the .NET **HttpListener** class, and then how to consume that service using PowerShell's REST cmdlets.

Creating Simple Web Service

PowerShell can host a lightweight web service by leveraging the .NET Framework's **HttpListener** class. This allows you to create a server that listens for HTTP requests and processes them based on custom logic. Below is a step-by-step guide to set up a simple web service that accepts parameters, performs a calculation, and returns a response.

Setting up Listener

Before you setup, first make surev the necessary .NET assemblies are loaded. In many cases, they are already available, but you can load additional ones if needed.

Then, create a new instance of the **HttpListener** and define the prefixes.

```
# Create and configure the HttpListener
$listener = New-Object System.Net.HttpListener
$listener.Prefixes.Add("http://localhost:8080/")
$listener.Start()
Write-Host "Web service is listening on
http://localhost:8080/"
```

This code initializes the listener and starts it, allowing it to accept incoming HTTP requests on port 8080.

Processing Incoming Requests

Here, first set up a loop to continuously listen for requests. Within the loop, extract query parameters, process them, and send a response.

```
while ($listener.IsListening) {
    try {
        # Get the incoming context (request/response pair)
        $context = $listener.GetContext()
        $request = $context.Request
        $response = $context.Response
        # Parse query parameters
        $queryParams =
[System.Web.HttpUtility]::ParseQueryString($request.Url.Query)
        $number1 = [int]$queryParams["number1"]
        $number2 = [int]$queryParams["number2"]
        # Perform a simple calculation (e.g., sum)
        $result = $number1 + $number2
        # Convert the result to bytes
        $buffer =
[System.Text.Encoding]::UTF8.GetBytes("Result: $result")
        $response.ContentLength64 = $buffer.Length
        # Write the response and close the stream
        $response.OutputStream.Write($buffer, 0,
$buffer.Length)
        $response.Close()
    }
    catch {
        Write-Warning "An error occurred: $_"
    }
}
```

This loop continuously processes incoming requests. It extracts two numbers from the query string, calculates their sum, and returns the result in the response.

Running Web Service

Next, save the script (e.g., as **web_service.ps1**) and run it in a PowerShell session. The service will start and listen for incoming HTTP requests. To test it, you can open a web browser or use PowerShell to send a request:

```
# Testing the web service with Invoke-RestMethod
$result = Invoke-RestMethod -Uri
"http://localhost:8080/?number1=10&number2=15" -Method Get
Write-Host $result
```

The above command sends a GET request with query parameters **number1=10** and **number2=15**, and displays the returned result, which should be "Result: 25".

Consuming Web Services

Once you have a web service running, consuming it is straightforward with PowerShell's REST cmdlets.

Using Invoke-RestMethod

The **Invoke-RestMethod** simplifies interaction with web services by automatically converting responses into PowerShell objects if the data is in JSON or XML format.

We first retrieve data from the web service by sending a GET request with the required parameters:

```
$uri = "http://localhost:8080/?number1=20&number2=30"
$response = Invoke-RestMethod -Uri $uri -Method Get
Write-Host "The result from the web service is: $response"
```

This command sends a GET request to your service and outputs the result, which in this case should be "Result: 50".

If your web service returns data in JSON or XML, **Invoke-RestMethod** will convert it automatically. For instance, if you modify your web service to return a JSON object:

```
# In your web service script, modify the response:
$jsonResponse = @{ result = $result } | ConvertTo-Json
$buffer = [System.Text.Encoding]::UTF8.GetBytes($jsonResponse)
```

```
$response.ContentLength64 = $buffer.Length
$response.OutputStream.Write($buffer, 0, $buffer.Length)
$response.Close()
```

Then, consuming it in PowerShell becomes:

```
$uri = "http://localhost:8080/?number1=20&number2=30"
$response = Invoke-RestMethod -Uri $uri -Method Get
Write-Host "The JSON result is: $($response.result)"
```

Using Invoke-WebRequest

For scenarios where you need detailed response information such as headers, cookies, or status codes, use **Invoke-WebRequest**. This cmdlet provides a more granular view of the HTTP response.

```
$response = Invoke-WebRequest -Uri
"http://localhost:8080/?number1=20&number2=30" -Method Get
Write-Host "HTTP Status: $($response.StatusCode)"
Write-Host "Response Headers: $($response.Headers)"
```

The **Invoke-WebRequest** is useful when you need to verify that your web service is behaving correctly or when you need to extract metadata from the HTTP response.

Summary

This chapter was all about making PowerShell's features better and making sure it can work well with different technologies. You learned to create custom extensions—ranging from functions and modules to full custom cmdlets—that tailor PowerShell to meet specific operational needs. You also explored how PowerShell can work with external systems, interacting with RESTful APIs, integrating with Python and Bash, and even creating and consuming web services. These advanced techniques let you link PowerShell with other platforms and tools, making it more useful in mixed environments and expanding its role in automating businesses.

Index

Epilogue

As I put the finishing touches on the "PowerShell SysAdmin Crash Course" (Second Edition), I find myself thinking about our shared journey. In this book, I've taken you through all kinds of topics, from the basics of PowerShell scripting to some pretty advanced stuff that takes it to the next level and lets you team it up with modern automation frameworks. Each chapter was designed to empower you to manage your IT environments with greater efficiency and confidence, and I hope that the hands-on examples and practical tips have inspired you to experiment, innovate, and streamline your day-to-day operations.

I remember how excited and helpful the feedback was, and it really helped shape this edition. I tried to address your needs by providing clear, actionable steps that not only simplify routine tasks but also prepare you for more complex challenges. The fact that this edition has evolved so much from the first one shows how dedicated we are to making things better and learning more. It's really satisfying to hear that a lot of you have been using these techniques in your own environments and changing up your system administration approach.

I encourage you to keep exploring and experimenting with PowerShell. The automation world is always changing, and the skills you've developed here will be a solid base for whatever challenges come your way in the future. Every new task is an opportunity to refine your approach and discover more efficient ways of working. No matter what you're doing, whether it's automating routine jobs, pushing updates across your network, or working with other automation tools, PowerShell's strength is in its flexibility and adaptability.

Your journey doesn't have to end here, though. I would like to invite you to share your experiences, contribute your insights, and even suggest improvements for future editions. Your feedback is super important for making this project better and better, and it helps us improve the techniques and tools that we're exploring together. As new versions of PowerShell and related technologies come out, there will always be more to learn and implement.

I'm super proud of the progress you've made and I'm stoked to see what challenges you'll overcome with your new skills. Keep building on these skills, automate with creativity, and push the boundaries of what's possible with PowerShell. Automation's not just about saving time — it's about letting you focus on what really matters and come up with new ideas that'll boost your organization.

The future looks bright, and I'm sure you'll find great success in your automation projects.

Thank You

www.ingramcontent.com/pod-product-compliance
Lightning Source LLC
Chambersburg PA
CBHW080242170726
48282CB00031B/1171
9789349174962